Leaders of Learning

By Rob Stokoe

A John Catt Publication

First Published 2014

by John Catt Educational Ltd,
12 Deben Mill Business Centre, Old Maltings Approach,
Melton, Woodbridge IP12 1BL

Tel: +44 (0) 1394 389850 Fax: +44 (0) 1394 386893
Email: enquiries@johncatt.com
Website: www.johncatt.com

© 2014 John Catt Educational Ltd

ISBN: 978 1 909717 220

Set and designed by John Catt Educational Limited

371.2012

Contents

About the author

With nearly 40 years experience within education, **Rob Stokoe** can both look back over a range of stimulating and challenging experiences and at an educational paradigm that has been subject to constant change.

It's fair to say that his career has been varied: 30 years leadership experience, including primary and secondary sectors; inspection and evaluation posts with Ofsted and the International Baccalaureate; five years as a senior lecturer at the University of Sunderland; and 14 years (and counting) leading the highly regarded Jumeirah English Speaking School in Dubai.

He has enjoyed the privilege of working alongside many gifted and dedicated educationalists that have inspired and informed his own growth – and is still, listening, learning and sharing, continually hoping to stimulate debate and growth for the most valuable of professions.

Other contributors

Ruth Burke, Head Teacher at Jumeirah English Speaking School, Dubai, is passionate about enriching learning opportunities for all children. Her 23 years of teaching and leading schools in Ireland, the UK and the UAE, as well as the experiences of raising her own three children (whose ages range from two to twenty), provide her with insight into a range of educational provision and quality. Whilst studying for her degree at Trinity College, Dublin she became very interested in leadership styles and subsequently completed a Masters' Degree in Educational Leadership from Bath University.

Shabnam Cadwallender is an ex-city girl from the North East of England, now part-time country wife and tenacious Head Teacher. Having served for 15 years in a range of primary schools as a class teacher, SENCO and senior leader, she now pushes the educational frontier as Head of a rural community school on the coast near Lancaster, England.

Preface

We are now well into the second decade of the 21st century. The ongoing evolution of our globally aware and connected society continues at a considerable pace, with sudden and all too frequent changes in direction. The demands and the potential for education are increasing and ever-changing, as are the requirements for leadership and leaders of learning. Despite the pace of change I believe we are living and working in the best of times. We now know so much more about how we learn, how our brains function and grow. Our collaborative networks are growing exponentially and educators are now globally connected. Furthermore there is a growing awareness and a deeper understanding emerging, a convergence of ideas, new and old, which are informing the educational debate.

We have a job to do: to make informed, considered decisions, to be flexible and proactive, take risks in order to structure and define ways of learning and inquiry-based education which will best meet the needs of students who are the greatest resource humanity has. Our goal is simply to determine a meaningful and purposeful future for each and every student globally.

I wish to offer my thanks to two talented educators who have offered chapters for this book, both of whom are currently in their first headship and have much to offer our profession. Ruth Burke is Head Teacher at Jumeirah English Speaking School, Dubai. She is a graduate of Trinity College, Dublin and Bath University, UK. Seema Anam is a graduate of the University of Sunderland, UK and Head Teacher of Caton CPS in Lancashire.

I continue to be humbled, filled with admiration and motivated by the vast contribution so many talented educators and thinkers are making to the context of learning at this time. Their meaningful work will make a difference. I am also aware that we all stand on the shoulders of giants, however if they enable us to see further then so be it. There is so much for us to do on every level in developing opportunities and equity for children globally. To this end, all of the personal proceeds from this book are being directed to the building of Mkuranga District Children's Home and Primary School in Tanzania initiated and supported by Larchfield Charity Organization.

For mum and dad for giving me the 'serenity to accept the things I cannot change, the courage to change the things I can, and the wisdom to know the difference' (Reinhold Niebuhr, 1892-1971).

Chapter 1

A 21st century curriculum: the advent of boutique education

The purpose of education is growth of individual potential. The function of teaching is to assist discovery, encourage creativity and to stimulate curiosity. For each of us our *raison d'etre* is to live our own life, a life that is engaging, challenging, safe and enjoyable. A curriculum for the 21st century must encourage the personal and intellectual growth of our young people; they are our greatest resource. A 'one size fits all' approach will not do. A highly personalised, skills and learner-focused experience for our students, a boutique curriculum, is required. In articulating a vision for great learning and teaching for our school, the learning pathway is an evolving framework of outcomes used to align pupil learning, personal development, curriculum, pedagogy, standards and assessment to support 21st century learning. Student outcomes within this boutique-style curriculum include skills and habits of mind with a clear focus upon the unique needs of learners, enhancing individual and collective capacity.

Inquiry-based learning is question-driven

The nurturing of curiosity in our students through the development of a thinking curriculum, where the search for questions far outweighs the search for answers is core to our work. In developing a child-centered curriculum infused with inquiry, we encourage our students to actively engage in rich learning experiences and in a learning paradigm that encourages independent and critical thinking to assist them in becoming powerful learners because '...powerful learners are curious' (Claxton, 2008).

There are no limits to a child's sense of wonder and curiosity and if we are focused upon growing individual potential, we require a curriculum which allows for greater flexibility. Our teachers, as effective knowledge professionals, have the role of creating an atmosphere where students feel comfortable about raising questions and curious and enthusiastic about facing and meeting challenges. We must 'leave the ideas, the solutions, the questioning and the excitement where it belongs, with our students' (Gentry & Ginnis, 2008).

Less often are we now focused upon 'pure' subjects, rather we engage with topics as a means of harnessing interest and promoting effective learning. How students learn is now given as much importance as what they learn. Each topic or project is treated differently, with consideration to thoughtful, connected and authentic ways to incorporate skills including critical thinking, problem solving, and communication and information literacy. Our goal is to create situations where our students love learning, seek challenges, value effort and persist in the face of difficulty. Our pedagogy and our learning context seek to develop secure, safe learners, actively engaged in a context which energises, stimulates curiosity and values open questioning.

Environments where it is 'hands up' to ask a question rather than to answer one

What students need to learn, how they learn and the sustainable quality of their learning is central to our curriculum. Goals within our curriculum define successful, intentional learners, self-aware individuals capable of continuously developing their capacity to learn, playing an active role in their own learning and demonstrating essential core skills in literacy and numeracy. As learners they will need to be creative, productive and discerning users of a variety of technologies in all areas of learning. Key skills will include the ability to think deeply and logically, to be creative, innovative and persistent in solving problems. Students are individually focused but have the ability and skills to work collaboratively, continually sharing and communicating their ideas and their thinking. Most importantly our intentional learners see connections in their learning; this drives them to know more. Projects centered on real life learning including entrepreneurship projects enable learners to amalgamate a wide variety of skills and disciplines with pupil, parent and staff voice feedback demonstrating an overwhelmingly positive response to the learning opportunities created. Alongside this we are continuing to focus upon personal attributes such as honesty, resilience and respect for others, each becoming confident and capable individuals with a strong sense of self worth.

Play must continue!

We need to build upon the strengths of the foundation stage curriculum which is providing an outstanding initial experience of school based education, strong on skills development with a clear focus upon experiential, social and collaborative learning in both formal and informal situations. There is a growing awareness of the need for greater coherence as we transition through key stages one, two and three. Thankfully the learning potential of play has extended well beyond the foundation stage, no longer is it viewed as a distraction or 'off-task' pursuit, rather a central driver for focused learning and exploration. 'To be playful and serious at the same time is possible, and it defines the ideal mental condition' (Dewey, 1910).

Core skills will always need to be strong

Our students will always need to read, to write and to calculate effectively. Reading, an abstract art and one of the most complex challenges in education, is central to achievement and the growth of our learners. We are continually striving to develop a positive disposition towards reading in our students; reading as a vital tool, not just for research but for the enjoyment of discovery and engagement with imagination. Furthermore, we are seeking to provide a context where our students listen carefully to and connect with the ideas of others, essentially encouraging the development of an empathetic learning style. This approach is actively supported by teachers who encourage questions, listen and facilitate the individual growth of each and every student - teachers who are as keen to learn as any child. The delivery of this style of curriculum requires highly skilled, confident and collaborative educators, dedicated to life-long learning and deeply committed to this whole school approach. Our diligent and innovative educators are the key drivers in supporting our young people who merit a more flexible and responsive curriculum, relevant to their unique learning and developmental needs.

Our curriculum is now interdisciplinary, project-based and research-driven

There is no question that the new technologies have changed the way our students learn. Technology has the potential to do many things, a new way to do old tasks or a way to make learning highly efficient and foster deeper levels of engagement and understanding. Clearly digital technologies have expanded the learning paradigm to a continuous learning experience. In creating an agile learning environment we are integrating an array of technologies, as powerful learning tools, in a coherent way that enriches the curriculum and enhances pedagogy, empowering learners and their learning.

We have a multitude of opportunities available to us; digital technology is empowering our curriculum and our learners, enabling learning and our classrooms to be boundless. eBooks provide opportunities to record, share and publish new knowledge as well as offering highly personalised feedback opportunities; pupils at our school have responded very favorably to audio feedback from teachers in their eBooks!

We are rapidly moving away from the mindset of teachers as content experts toward the concept of learning which is subject to discussion, questioning and negotiation rather than one of imposition. This enhancement of the teacher's role is enabling our students to navigate the wide array of resources available to them. Students are encouraged to seek out knowledge, to discriminate effectively, to effectively use resources to support the acquisition of new knowledge and skills.

This new knowledge constructed through research and application is more often linked to real life situations and previous experiences. With support from our educators, students skilfully organize new information, constantly refreshing and renewing their thinking, continuously growing their potential. Assessment is now focused on differentiated experiences and outcomes with success criteria effectively scaffolding students' learning.

An evolving process of growing a learning culture that values rich discussion and focuses upon students' questions is well underway. Our belief is that the quality of discussion, the critical act of questioning and the active listening role of the teacher combine to encourage intellectual confidence and personal growth for our students. Our students are positive, willing learners who openly accept challenge and are confident in a discovery context.

The development of science discovery corners, for instance, allow students in the early years not only to dress up and act like scientists but to explore and demonstrate their natural curiosity as they encounter new materials and experiences. Carefully selected materials inform new challenges where the questions raised during their exploration are the intended outcome of the activity. Teachers are planning for inquiry, tapping into student curiosity and the sense of wonder within each child, carefully developing opportunities for them to organize their learning in such a way that it supports the ongoing acquisition of skills, knowledge and attitudes at their individual level and pace of learning.

Effective educators within our school are promoting focused discussion, actively listening to students and encouraging questioning; it is really interesting to watch high quality teachers resisting the temptation to talk! Teachers are intentionally modelling key learning attributes including enthusiasm, engagement, listening and sensitivity.

Great timing is key in this process; selecting the right question at the right time, offering questions that are open-ended to promote thinking and pupil-led learning takes intentional practice. Learning pathways are often semi-structured allowing teachers to plan, think and respond flexibly, allowing for varying pace which supports the individual learner or group. The most interesting challenge encountered in the context of this boutique-style education is that in some cases learning will not have a clearly defined end point.

The 21st century curriculum has developed as project-based, research-driven and interdisciplinary with students and educators collaborating in the pursuit of learning within and beyond the classroom. Our educators, fantastic orchestrators of learning, are enriching the lives of our students as they engage them in developing an integrated knowledge base, alongside positive habits of mind and enabling them as happy, confident life-long learners. As educators we exist to help students grow, learn and achieve, to discover their unique talents, and it is outstanding learning and teaching which underpins every effective school, whatever the century.

References and further reading

Claxton, G. (2008). *What's the Point of School: Rediscovering the Heart of Education.* Oxford: Oneworld

Dewey, J. (1910) *How we think.* Massachusetts: D. C. Heath and Company

Gentry, J. W. & McGinnis, L. P. (2008) *Thoughts on How to Motivate Students Experientially. Developments in Business Simulation and Experiential Learning,* 35, p.73-77

Hargreaves, A. & Fullan, M. (2012) *Professional Capital: Transforming Teaching in Every School.* New York: Teachers College Press

Kashdan, T. (2009) *Curious? Discover the Missing Ingredient to a Fulfilling Life.* William Morrow

Shenk, D. (2010) *The Genius in All of Us: Why Everything You've Been Told about Genetics, Talent, and IQ Is Wrong.* Doubleday

Chapter 2

Leaders of schools: architects of learning

We are living in times of challenge and opportunity where continual uplift of outcomes is a requirement of continuous improvement. As educational leaders we exercise high level of influence over our core functions of learning and teaching. To that end we set ambitious targets and rigorously monitor student progress over time, based upon evidence.

Our professional responsibility is to be informed, supportive and available to assist growth, constantly encouraging and developing the way our teachers think, the way they teach to constantly build an empowering culture. By deliberately driving for a better tomorrow, by motivating and developing our educators we can have a positive influence upon student learning and achievement. This lies at the very heart of effective school leadership: leadership which is focused upon providing challenge and guidance, where all stakeholders are involved in making a positive impact upon learning for the benefit of every student.

High performing educational leaders develop a compelling vision, have clarity of purpose and drive for the excellence of both experience of learning and outcome for every student; they are persuasive in sharing that purpose. They have the courage to offer challenge and believe that their ability to inspire, build capacity and self confidence will make a difference. They are clock builders not timekeepers.

In informing and defining a better future for every student the following steps are imperative:

- Agree and define a vision, one which articulates a better future for every student.
- Define and communicate a pathway, the milestones and the educational context of that challenge.
- Model and share the pedagogical requirement, the challenge for every teacher, the expert traits you are seeking to develop.
- Engage in the debate, the knowledge sharing, defining the measurable outcomes, ensuring that innovations are connected to your vision and mission.
- Define the monitoring and recognising process, assuring the quality of understanding, of impact and outcome.

Diversity of roles and styles

Effectively all educational leaders adopt a number of diverse roles and leadership styles in dealing with the complexity of school life and the perpetual challenge of moving a school forward. Many see themselves as transformational leaders with a strong focus upon the relationship between leaders and followers, a useful trait; however it is not a predictive of the quality of student's outcomes (Robinson, Lloyd & Rowe, 2008) In managing the conditions for learning effective leaders build the desire to become better for the good of learners; inspiring collective growth and effort from all staff.

Learning-focused leadership is directly engaged with learning and teaching where active, engaged lead educators demonstrate their passion for learning and pupils' advancement. This involved leadership brings a clear focus to learning which informs student growth, continually developing their potential in a way which is both inspirational and challenging for the teaching communities we lead. It is a model founded in vision, communication and demandingness as we continuously offer agendas for professional growth and improvement toward a common goal of excellence. After all a great school is no more than a series of great classrooms.

The bonding agent that holds these classrooms together is a shared appreciation of excellent teaching, how we progress pupil learning and how that learning should be evaluated. Alongside this high quality evaluations carried out by knowing leaders and peers are essential in informing improvement in teaching and student outcomes. They are especially effective when teachers see feedback as developmental and 'useful'.

Inspect what you expect

The most effective school leaders bring a thorough appreciation of learning and teaching; developing a context where there is never uncertainty about expectation and the quality of a teacher's work. They inspect what they expect. One of our greatest challenges is to marry the diverse challenges of quality assurance and their potential to positively influence teachers thinking and level of engagement to the schools vision and mission. Accountability for outcomes and quality assurance as well as the leadership responsibility for it are simply facts of life. In effect we are not there to support the notion of absolute autonomy of any teacher; the predispositions of an individual educator cannot undermine the collective capacity of your team.

Learning leaders need to give consideration to a 21st century appreciation of learning and teaching especially the impact of digital and inquiry-based learning. We support educators to come to terms with a critical awareness that pedagogies require continual re examination and that what we do with knowledge is more important than mere acquisition of knowledge. There is a note of caution here as it's not just about new strategies; it's about making a difference. We need to secure evidence about the impact and outcomes of such strategies.

Professional learning

For the successful 21st century school, which is inspirational for its teaching community, there needs to be a clear focus upon professional learning. There cannot be a disconnect between leadership purpose and the drive to improve the quality of learning and teaching in every classroom. Students are forever at the heart of an effective school, with the true purpose of our leadership being the drive to make best practice common practice, ensuring that each and every student receives the highest quality of education and the opportunity to succeed. Clearly communicated learning leadership will bring a clear focus to the impact of the learning and teaching process and connection to student outcomes. As stated in Hattie (2009): 'School leaders who focus on student achievement and instructional (learning) strategies are the most effective.' Clearly when leaders focus their expertise, energy and talent pool upon pedagogical growth and student achievement the outcome has a positive measurable impact. Learning leaders can nurture and develop the knowledge and skills and positive attitudes which will inform great learning and sustainable change.

Great schools require leadership which communicates confidently, demands and facilitates life-long learning. Leaders will constantly motivate highly engaged educators to be flexible and responsive, contributing to the continual drive to improve pedagogy across the school knowing that as a consequence you will constantly uplift student achievement.

A key role for any leader is to model, instigate and promote collegial discussions about learning, to encourage reflection and a continuous open dialogue upon great teaching. Furthermore it will be important to negotiate a structured learning pathway for every educator, allowing them to continually develop a broader and deeper knowledge of learning and to contribute to the continuous improvement of the school.

Teachers will develop skills well beyond basic competencies and will know when and how to intervene to support learning, even when not to intervene, based upon knowledge, evidence and experience. As stated in Dufour & Marzano (2011), 'there is considerable evidence that when teachers work together on the right work, even for as little as one hour each week, we can expect gains in student achievement'.

Differentiation and personalisation

As we strive to achieve the highest standards for all we will develop meaningful discussions relating to areas such as differentiation and personalisation of learning we will identify and share excellent practice, developing opportunities for staff to witness, share and grow alongside their colleagues. We will need informed learning leaders who can identify expert teachers or expert traits within teachers, who can model outstanding practice, expert teachers who can make their thinking visible (Darling-Hammond & Borat-Smith, 2005); teachers who have mastery and purpose.

Assessment of student work scrutinised against clear learning intentions lies at the heart of the teaching and learning cycle. A learning leader is tasked with identifying and sharing effective strategies, ensuring moderation against a background of evidence-based decision-making. This will allow teachers to scaffold learning and inform positive developmental opportunities for students in thoughtfully-constructed learning environments which develop appropriate opportunities for all students.

We serve our schools as leaders of leaders, accepting that we are living in times of challenge where continual uplift of outcomes is a requirement. Leaders are there to make a difference, accepting that, 'a highly effective school leader can have a dramatic influence on the overall academic achievement of students' (Fullan, 2005). To that end leaders must demonstrate constancy of purpose toward improvement, set ambitious targets and rigorously monitor student progress over time.

In communicating a fundamental belief that all students can learn and grow; they provide intellectual leadership and continually drive for growth in teacher skill, performance as well as student outcomes. The learning leader is an encourager, an active participant in the study of teaching and learning and a facilitator of collaborative efforts amongst teachers. In the best instances they establish carefully selected coaching relationships with and between teachers. This is all done with a clear focus upon uplifting student achievement.

As leaders we are most effective when we work collaboratively toward clear common goals, accepting that student learning is at the centre of everything we do. We share and distribute leadership, both individual and shared, seeking to develop the leadership of everyone in the school, including our students. Great leaders are architects of learning who know where the best learning and teaching is happening in their schools. They then provide the opportunity to showcase these beacons of excellence to learning peers, constantly encouraging the development of strategies for positive intervention to inform learning. They apply understanding from available data effectively, systematically monitoring progress. These leaders are explicit in their expectations as they continually challenge, taking learning forward for the betterment of all concerned, especially our students. The real significance of learning leadership is that it makes a difference and recognises that great teaching matters, a lot. It is great teaching that ultimately will impact so positively upon the development of confident, resilient learners and subsequent school success. We know that we do not have all the answers at this time, but we know enough to start the conversation.

References and further reading

Darling-Hammond, L. & J. Baratz-Snowden (2005) *A Good Teacher in Every Classroom.* San Francisco, CA: John Wiley & Sons

Dinham S. (2012) *Walking the Walk, The need for school leaders to embrace teaching as a clinical practice profession.* University of Melbourne

DuFour, R. & Marzano, R. J. (2011) *Leaders of Learning: How District, School, and Classroom Leaders Improve Student Achievement.* Bloomington: Solution Tree

Fullan M. (2005) *Leadership & Sustainability: Systems Thinkers in Action.* Thousand Oaks, CA: Corwin Press

Hattie J. (2009) *Visible Learning.* London: Routledge

Robinson, V. M. J., Lloyd, C. A., & Rowe, K. J. (2008) The impact of leadership on school outcomes: *Educational Administration Quarterly,* 44(5), 635-674

Chapter 3

Building a school within a school

Today schools are integrated and interdisciplinary with a clear focus upon a student-centered learning context. New technologies are infused into learning. Our classrooms have become global and we are developing collaborative life-long learners as we shift the curriculum in order that we do all we can to ensure that our young people are equipped to meet the challenges to find success in the 21st century.

A life-long journey
Leading a school in this context provides a unique paradigm; there is never an ultimate destination, only the journey and that's life-long. As leaders we know what our schools stand for; we inform school renewal and improvement, facilitate quality teaching, student achievement, constantly improving who we are. As leaders we bring positive attitudes which are contagious, intellectual capacity, a bias to risk-taking as we are open to change, and opportunity. We offer strong moral leadership: we support, feedback; we listen to our staff and treat them professionally seeking a high level of professionalism in return. After all if you think you're leading and no-one is following, then you're only taking a walk.

Understanding the unique context of your school is of critical importance. The yesterday, today and tomorrow are all clearly linked and interdependent. Change is also impacted by industrial and political expectation, the growing understanding we have of the nature of intelligence and the students themselves. How do you ensure that your school has the capacity for change? The resilient nature of any organisation to inform continuous improvement and sustains growth is critical. Several key elements are necessary in developing a foundation for a better future:

- Strong, creative, consistent strategic leadership;
- Continually clarifying and deepening of a clearly articulated vision;
- A passion and dedication to succeed in creating a better future; and
- The continuing growth of the individual and collective capacity of the teachers.

Capacity building

Clearly you need to determine to what extent the factors are in place are central to your leadership; this is the foundation of future orientated capacity building. Ensuring that effective structures are in place is a critical function of leadership, allowing you to 'know' your school. This is your internal Inheritance, the moral purpose of your school a starting point from which you create energy , build capacity, secure and enhance the environment, seek and chart improvement, extend the vision of what is possible.

As a leader once you know your school you can define and articulate the journey beyond your current requirements, your journey from vision to mission. A sustainable journey focused upon continuous improvement for the benefit of every student where the entire school has a focus upon continual learning for all. This initial stage of structure building, of knowing may be referred to as moderation or quality assurance; it is a process that lies at the heart of developing your professional learning community. As leaders we need to evaluate, assess and plan on the basis of evidence. The collection of this evidence and monitoring is about improvement.

Leadership is a verb, and to be a leader you must be a continual learner, a strategic thinker, value and vision-driven; a learning coach and a builder of learning structures. We need a clear awareness, an understanding of what works in learning, not fad or ideology

Arriving at a shared understanding of standards involves leaders at all levels within the school. It involves building strong reciprocal relationships and a culture of interdependency. Effective leadership can determine a strong professional expectation for all, one which can be measured and developed – developing strengths shared across the school community. Leadership is the enabler as we determine and articulate clear expectations about the acceptable approaches to and quality in the pedagogy offered to students, developmental and clearly differentiated.

This approach will exemplify and build upon standards in planning, learning, teaching and assessment, to improve performance. In order to know our schools we need to know the detail, checking, sampling, agreeing where students are and their next steps in learning and sharing this with them is not negotiable.

Collaboration and skill acquisition

Feedback is the breakfast of champions. Communicating feedback and encouraging collaboration with and between colleagues is imperative, as you identify and share potential improvements in practices which will inform student learning and their developing life skills which will positively inform their futures. Developmental feedback of this nature offers educators profoundly different learning contexts for skill acquisition against a background of collaboration and continual improvement whilst maintaining continuity of focus upon student learning and achievement.

Involving and informing teachers, assisting their professional growth in a collaborative and meaningful way is a highly effective form of professional development. Leaders should never underestimate what they have to offer in terms of defining innovative responses, consistent communication and building great teams as a shared vision emerges from a personal vision.

Quality assurance and moderation must always be both rigorous and robust, they are after all accountability procedures, but at the same time it must foster mutual trust, openness to different ideas and respect for the different skills, experience and understanding that participants bring. Ultimately the aim is to ensure that learning, teaching and assessment is planned in a thoughtful and coherent way and that assessment is consistent and integral to learning and teaching. Efficient, consistent and effective approaches to quality assurance and moderation will continually build upon current practices building ever stronger working approaches to learning and teaching. Ever stronger opportunities for professional dialogue can be cultured with supportive feedback and elements such as peer mentoring energizing professional development.

Continuity and flow of experience

Dialogue and pace of change are key components. Faster may be slower, as the harder you enforce change the greater the likelihood of resistance. Know the optimal growth rate of your teams. Such approaches will promote capacity building; strengthen your professional learning community. Over time your school will arrive at a shared understanding with educators sharing their expertise and innovation for the benefit of all as you build upon existing standards and expectations.

There are challenges, getting the balance right between challenge and sustainability as we reaffirm expectations encouraging teachers to engage in challenging and engaging learning experiences focused upon informing the progress of every student. There is also the greatest challenge of getting the balance right across the key points of transition through a curriculum, we should always be seeking a flow of experience which supports our students in the most positive and effective way. It will support teachers as they will have greater confidence in assessment judgments and the reliability of information which informs their planning for student progression at the next stage in learning.

Continuity and secure progression building upon previous learning is everything to an effective school. When combined with monitoring or moderation structures working across the school focused upon raising quality and learning opportunities and decreasing the variation from classroom to classroom this is a powerful force for growth. This requires a highly professional approach with high levels of commitment to change and educators who embrace both challenge and accountability, is it worthwhile of course because as a leader you are the person who has 'the capacity to translate vision into reality' (Warren Bennis).

Every step of the way that reality brings focus to providing better experiences for students who are always our primary consideration, students who must be challenged and stretched to become what they may be.

Vision and mission: meaningful, inspirational and purposeful?

While there are many factors that interact to constitute an effective school, Collins (2001) maintains that there are two critical factors that differentiate 'great' from 'good' schools: the existence of a compelling vision and effective leadership. The purpose of leadership is to inspire and enlist others on our journey. A vision which is meaningful and compelling is essential as it is a declaration of a shared purpose, expressing ideas about an agreed future. It is vision which gives purpose to a school, its reason for existence, defining core values and the strategic intent, a stretch goal outlining future aspirations. Ultimately a vision ceases to become an idea; it evolves to become a force for change driven by the professional attributes and passion of the school community.

In setting this context for action the purpose of the school should be clearly reflected and easily accessed through its vision and mission statements which should enhance workplace meaning, the why and how we do things, demonstrating that we understand our beliefs. We then need to articulate and involve staff in discussing and finalising statements; this will further engage teachers, as they strive for purposeful and meaningful learning on a daily basis.

All staff should experience the connection, the relationship between such statements and the daily workings of our schools. Stassens and Vandenberghe (1994) clearly note that vision and mission statements provide meaning to teachers work and have the potential to have a positive impact on their motivation. We need statements that make a difference, encourage collegiality, inform a culture of great learning experience, success, continuous improvement and foster a belief that learning is for everyone and never stops. It must also reflect our willingness to take risks as well as a sense of interdependence, and care and mutual respect (adapted from Day, 1999)

The educational personality of schools

As effective leaders we are able to shape the 'educational personality' of schools. Within this the challenge is the pursuit of an educational ideal, defining a desired future for your school. The definition of a clear compelling and inspirational vision statement founded in the value system of any school is critical and meaningful. The first stage in our thinking must

23

be to explore, discuss and internalise the real meanings of vision, mission and values statements for JESS. We need to comprehend the interplay between transformational and moral leadership and our commitment to continual improvement for our school, our students and our educators. A first step in understanding these complex relationships is to understand what 'work' means to teachers: what teachers expect from their work and what motivates them. Each of us has our own sense of identity tied up in our work, after all both leading and teaching can become a way of acting out our personal values. This is especially complex against a background of intensification from change that is both rapid and constant.

Meaningful work and belonging to a vision enables individuals to 'belong to something bigger than themselves' (Limmerick, Cunnington and Crowther, 2002). Most people aspire to this. It enables them to share values, enable positive interactions to grow professionally against a background of sharing and integration of practice. Our leadership can inform and energise these processes to grow human capital, organisational consistency and capacity. Owens (2001) reminds us about the goals of leadership, stating that the goal of leadership is to build human capital: to energise and unite and motivate others through unity of purpose.

Most teachers agree that values are an important part of any organisation and have the potential to impact constructively upon how we act and feel. In selecting your teachers and leaders, you are informing a culture. Deal (1985) writes: 'At the heart of most definitions of culture is the concept of a learned pattern of unconscious (or semi-conscious) thought reflected and re-enforced by behaviour that powerfully and silently shapes the experience of people' (p. 301).

However it is in the development of a common moral purpose which will drive increased motivation of our staff through a genuine sharing of values, aspirations and ambition. As staff commit to this common strand and commit to personal growth we will further grow the potential of our school with a staff who will display higher levels of competence, engagement and ultimately success.

The National College for School Leadership (NCSL) (2005) suggests the 'need for teacher leaders to develop people and be person-centred, putting a premium on professional relationships and build trust and collaborative ways of working throughout the school'.

Will any vision statement make a difference? The answer is no, as a collection of words in itself cannot do anything. It will not enhance engagement, understand, enhance trust, build teacher commitment or inform student learning. The real power of any vision statements lies in the creation, empowerment, and implementation life of that vision. The leader's role then becomes clear: the processes should be such that they build a culture of interdependency enabling teachers to collectively apply these values to their work in classrooms. They should inspire teachers. Aspirant 21st century educational leaders will need to inspire those we lead by establishing, implementing and assessing an attractive, worthwhile, achievable vision of the future for your school.

Vision will always equate with challenge as it is an invitation to a better future! It represents a future that is beyond what is possible today or what we think possible tomorrow. Always reflecting the unique context of your environment a vision is grounded in and an extension of the history, the current reality, culture and values of the school. What we stand for never changes, yet how we do things is subject to continual change and that is both challenging and motivational. Remember that none of us is as good as all of us as you strive to meet the challenge of building capacity and connectedness in a community of learning and practice. Have the courage to embrace the notion of building a school within a school, enjoy the journey.

References and further reading

Collins J. (2001) *Good to Great: Why Some Companies Make the Leap...And Others Don't.* Harper Collins

Day, C. (1999) *Developing Teachers: the Challenges of Lifelong Learning.* London: Falmer Press

Deal, T. E. (1985). Cultural change: opportunity, silent killer or metamorphosis? In R. H. Kilman, Saxton, M. J. and Sherpa, R. (eds), *Gaining control of corporate culture.* San Francisco: Jossey-Bass

Limmerick, D., Cunnington, B. & Crowther, F. (2002). *Managing the new organisation: collaboration and sustainability.* Crows Nest, NSW: Allen and Unwin

Louis, K. S. (2007) Trust and improvement in schools. *Journal of Educational Change,* 8(1), 1-24

National College for School Leadership. (2005). Learning-centred leadership; towards personalised learning-centred leadership. Nottingham: National College for School Leadership

Owens, R. G. (2001). *Organisational behaviour in education: instructional leadership and school reform* (7th ed.). Boston: Allyn and Bacon

Staessens, K. & Vandenberghe, R. (1994). *Vision as a core component in school culture.* Journal of Curriculum Studies, 26(2), 187-200

Chapter 4

Curiosity and creativity: conditions for learning

'Never trust a man who, when left alone in a room with a tea cozy, doesn't try it on.'
Billy Connolly (1994)

In the words of Thomas Edison, *'the greatest invention in the world is the mind of a child'*, and every mind is born with the instinct of curiosity. We all come into the world curious and creative: innate gifts. As young children, we are wonderfully creative and curious about everything. Curiosity and creativity are natural, inquisitive behaviours that engender exploration, investigation and learning (Wikipedia, 2014). It is an openness to experience new things, trying to find answers to the whys that we've asked and continue to ask throughout our lives. Yet research tells us that both creativity and curiosity declines as we progress through our education systems.

Curiosity: the unrestricted desire to understand

The fact is that young people are curious about everything; *they have an unrestricted desire to understand* (Henman, 2009). At five years of age 98% of all children have no problem thinking divergently. Not surprising really, three-year-olds, on average, ask their parents about 100 questions a day, every day! However by the time they are ten to 11 years of age they've pretty much stopped asking. Of even greater concern is that by the age of 25 only 2% can think outside the box. Curiosity seldom survives into adulthood (Keen, 1973).

As we grow up, we start believing the answers are more important than the questions. Yet adult creativity is still powerful, there is just not enough of it. It can be said that the creative adult is the curious child who survived. Fostering the scholarly attribute of curiosity in learners is an important task; one which is at the heart of education and effective learning as it challenges and promotes active participation in learning.

As educators our challenge is that curiosity and curriculum are antithetical concepts with the curriculum often acting to limit student empowerment rather than enable for the most part. As educators we need to embrace curiosity and discovery in our thinking and planning. However, this is easier said than done, predominantly the curriculum dictates the teacher's planning rather than the individual ideas or questions of the student. Our deliberate and thoughtful consideration and actions have the potential to empower our students, provoking and extending their engagement, learning and thinking. We need to plan in a thoughtful and purposeful way, creating an environment of possibility where the concept of the child as the architect of their own knowledge is valued and built upon. In essence we will be attempting continually inspire not require. The reality is that curiosity is the driving force behind life-long learning as Gentry and McGinnis (2008) argue, learning to learn (or to be curious) is the most essential skill that they can acquire.

Curiosity creates learning

Curiosity and discovery never age and are so powerful that they create learning; continually building upon itself, allowing our minds to open up as they grow and develop. Why is curiosity so important? We would all agree that curiosity instigates intellectual activity and is a central ingredient to a fulfilling life (Kashdan, 2009). Our purpose must be to nurture curiosity in our students, and to do this we will be required to develop a thinking curriculum which requires the verbalising of questions, a curriculum where the search for questions far outweighs the search for answers. Therefore curiosity becomes the cutting edge of knowledge, which is not in the knowing, it is in the questioning (adapted from Thompson,

1969) Educational growth and the excitement of learning are not confined to the powers of recall, it is not about knowing what is, but creating a greater expectation of deeper learning and a higher level of understanding; it demands that we all aspire to be better than we thought we could be.

The important thing for all students is not to stop questioning because what is essential for their current and future learning is the ability to ask questions. The acquisition of knowledge and learning derives its energy through questioning. If we are to affect real learning, which can never be a one-way channel, learning must be an interaction between the teacher and the student. We must step away from any consideration that it is time-consuming to foster a student inquiry; it is actually time efficient in that it has the potential to inform learning within and beyond school, supporting anytime, anywhere, life-long and life-wide learning.

All active learners need the freedom to question and we need to encourage them to initiate more often. When we embrace the notion that questioning is a special kind of learning we will engage our students in the intellectual process of questioning more often. Research has indicated that students stop asking questions over time. Students don't stop asking questions because they lose interest, it's the other way around; they lose interest because they stop asking questions.

Curiosity ties in well with enquiry based learning, which is essential to a well balanced curriculum. In order for this to happen we need to foster confidence in our students so that they feel that they can be curious. They should never apologise for asking a question. Put simply, there is no such thing as a stupid question; only one which hasn't been asked! We need to teach our students that it's okay to ask questions when you don't know/ understand something, or even just to generate a discussion. They must not stop asking questions.

In addition, we must assure that our curricula allows for questioning and open-mindedness. When will all education systems come to terms with the notion that we must incorporate more independent thought instead of requiring students to simply memorise facts?

Creative thinking: our edge

Creativity is a gift in each of us; it is a flame that burns within us, making every one of us special and unique. We recognise and value creativity as way of life acknowledging that any 'new' idea is no more than a combination of known elements. As stated by Einstein (1879-1955), 'the secret to creativity is knowing how to hide your sources'. Schools and the curricular offered often feature logical, linear thinking an essential life skill.

It's 'in the box' thinking. It may have been useful in the past; however, for 21st century success you also need creative, big picture thinking. We need to be able to think outside of the box. Creativity is about using your whole brain, your entire talent and this is what needs to be accessed and developed in our classrooms. Our children need to be curious, playful, constantly challenged; we want everyone to be a genius, at least once a year.

Creativity is the seed of innovation; the threat here is that we allow creativity to be curbed because we are focused upon learning and thinking which is linear, too often based around facts and the needs of the curriculum rather than the individual. We need to think the way a child thinks – no restrictions, no fear – and only then will we give real value to innovation and creativity, ensuring that education fulfils its intentions: to prepare the workforce of tomorrow for a future that has not been written.

The best educators provide learning environments that protect and encourage students to approach learning and thinking this way; this approach encourages creativity, and happier, more successful learners as children remain open to challenges and new ideas. All students have the potential and ability to be creative; we just need to give them the opportunity to think creatively. In return we will see students who have greater ownership of their learning, demonstrate higher levels of interest and work well with others. Today creativity is viewed as a practical skill, one which can be taught and will enable students to problem solve more effectively.

All humans have the potential and ability to be creative. Curiosity and creativity are essential elements and can be infused into in a well-rounded education. Where and when do we begin? Firstly, creativity is not limited to the arts, people are inherently creative. Fostering creativity clearly has long-term positive benefits, our initial focus will be in the early years ensuring that this focus is maintained even when the curriculum is subject to end of stage assessments and the opinions of others have greater influence as well as an increasingly crowded curriculum, when the need to know the right answer becomes important. The challenge for educators is to find the space to continue to nurture creativity against the pressure of curriculum delivery. We can promote creativity in our learners by actively encouraging their questions as well as providing problem-solving opportunities.Students will always require opportunities to explore and discuss their own ideas as well as continual challenge, even in this context the stress of failure can provide opportunities to learn. Our questioning should continue to be challenging and open ended and we must assure that assessment continues to recognise discovery, creativity and innovation.

Creativity in early years science

As educators we want our students to ask lots of questions, to make connections in their learning, to enjoy discovery. Simple changes in our thinking can bring about positive changes in the way we encourage students to participate in the learning process. We want our classrooms to be dynamic places that encourage active learning, where learning is engaging and accessible to everyone.

Instead of having a science corner, why not create a scientists' corner? A place where students can experience science, raise their own questions, make connections and build upon previous knowledge, exchange their ideas. This activity zone will support and empower learners by allowing them to take control of their learning as a greater emphasis is put on discovery and experiential learning. Experiments don't need to be complicated; students can experiment safely investigating in a context akin to play. They dress as scientists, experience new challenges, building upon the role modeling offered by their teachers.

Scientists behave the way children of all ages do; they ask questions, they observe the world around them. They collect and discuss new information in order to seek answers. Teachers encourage and stimulate their students' natural interest in their surroundings seeking to give them an authentic science experience. The quality and variety of language that pupils hear and speak are key factors in developing their scientific vocabulary; behaving as scientists and sharing their findings will assist in making their thinking clear, both to themselves and others.

The use of language is central to the notion 'working like a scientist', allowing time to share, discuss and compare ideas. Science education can be factually based; however it is of greater importance for the learner to discover these facts themselves through the use of talk and exploration.

It is our responsibility to make sure that our natural curiosity, compassion and creativity are not left behind. The best educators would wish to work in schools which encourage independent learning and gives value to curiosity and creativity. As leaders it is our responsibility to ensure that natural curiosity, compassion and creativity are central to our students learning experience. As educators we have a direct impact on student performance, it is our function to maintain creativity and curiosity and actively support student inquiry as much as it is to deliver any given curriculum. If not will we continue to be guilty of unintentional neglect? (Henman, 2009).

All too often we are missing the opportunity to cultivate the individual's quest in favour of curriculum delivery and the need to get through schemes of work. More often we need to adopt thinking around mutual respect within our learning environments as well as actively listening to our students. We need to create contexts where creativity and curiosity stimulates situations where active participants embrace the mode of inquiry. Where teachers facilitate or guide collaborative or individual learning rather than maintain the teacher as the focus of it. As educators we must satisfy student curiosity with explanation and offer opportunities which support creativity, creating learning environments which are continuously accepting of and encouraging both.

Nourish each learner's creativity, curiosity and sense of wonder

As highly valued knowledge professionals, we create incredible learning for others. As learning leaders we generate human growth, learning and cultivate ideas. To be what we can be as educators our primary role must be to maintain, to nourish, and to celebrate each learner's individual creativity and their curiosity and sense of wonder. Every day we need to create an atmosphere where students feel comfortable about taking a chance, trying something new, raising questions and let our students know that their questions are not only valued, but have an important place in our learning environments. We can be highly responsive to our students needs and continuously challenge students to develop skills and gain new knowledge and understanding.

Within our classrooms we need to nurture a genuine attitude of exploration and deep interest in everything, ways of thinking and being. This has the potential for our students to become more confident and flexible, adaptable and active learners. Creative, curious people will learn how to learn and repeat the process again and again. As often as possible, we want to leave the ideas, the solutions, the suggestions, the purpose, the questioning, and the excitement where it belongs — with our students.

Activities which allow more student choice and individual expression are a start. We can encourage students to learn through active exploration. Encourage questions such as, 'What would happen if...?' We can also model creativity and curiosity, ask questions, engage in exploration alongside students to resolve the questions they pose, we can demonstrate our enthusiasm for both.

Maybe we just need to stand back and ask ourselves the question: Are we like our students, are we driven by the unrestricted desire to understand? By personalising the experience of learning for each student we can encourage them to connect with their own intellectual passions, as well as providing authentic relationships between educators and learners. By focusing upon their creativity and curiosity we will continually encourage their desire to learn.

Daily we will have the opportunity to inspire our students, to make them engaged and independent learners. Put simply, if we want to improve the quality of our students' thinking we must learn to support them in improving the quality of their questions and their creativity.

Ultimately we will engender in our charges more active and reflective thinking, happy learners in classrooms driven by passion, creativity, curiosity, and the occasional dream. If you tell me that curiosity killed the cat ... I would say that curiosity was framed! Creativity and curiosity merit our attention.

References and further reading

Arnone, Marilyn P., (2003) Using Instructional Design Strategies to Foster Curiosity

Bronson, P. & Merryman, A., (2010); The creativity crisis. *Newsweek*. Available at www.thedailybeast.com/newsweek/2010/07/10/ the-creativity-crisis.html

Gentry, J.W. & McGinnis, L.P. (2008); Thoughts on how to motivate students experientially. *Developments in Business Simulation and Experiential Learning.* 35: 73-77

Henman, R. (2009) The functional relationship between Curiosity and collaboration

Kashdan, T. B., (2009) *Curious? Discover the missing ingredient to a fulfilling life.* New York: William Morrow

Keen, S. (1973) *Apology for Wonder.* New York: Harper & Row, p. 58

Land, G. & Jarman, B. (1993) *Breaking Point and Beyond.* San Francisco: HarperBusiness

Loewenstein, G. (1994); The psychology of curiosity: A review and reinterpretation. *Psychological Bulletin.* 116(1): 75-98

Richardson, E. S. (1964) Teaching as a Creative Art in the Early World. NZCER

Schwitzgebe, E. (1996) Theories in Children and the Rest of Us. *Philosophy of Science.* 63

Thompson, R. (1969); Learning to Question. *The Journal of Higher Education.* 40(6)

Turak, A. (2011) Steve Jobs and the One Trait All Innovative Leaders Share. *Forbes*

Chapter 5

Building capacity, sustainability and happy learners

First act like a leader, for true leadership
is not in one's position, but in one's
way of thinking and acting it is in the
nobility of one's objectives and goals.
(Mohammed bin Rashid Al Maktoum, 2013)

We must always acknowledge that as leaders, our primary responsibility is to create a happy, positive, learning culture where students, staff, and parents are safe, and all understand the significant role they have to play. A successful school must be a happy place.

Leadership: a duality

As leaders, we inform school renewal and improvement, we facilitate quality teaching and student achievement, constantly improving whom we are, setting clear, agreed, high standards; creating a culture, an expectation of success. Our leadership sets the tone; we must be inspirational, honest, and forward-thinking, know when to consult and when to be decisive; at all times courageous. The duality of leadership will always challenge us: the first challenge is to be managerial, to control the operation of the school; the second being to create a vision which promotes development and change. We need to be decisive in our decision-making yet demonstrate humility, a strategic thinker yet a master of detail, focused in our drive for excellence but also collaborative, an effective listener.

The following will always support leaders well: maintain student learning at the heart of the school, think creatively, act flexibly, value and engage with people, understand and manage risks, deliver. Leadership philosophy evolves; it develops over time, responding to daily challenges and new paradigms. We need a clear awareness, an understanding, of what works in learning, a bias towards innovation yet on a daily basis we must exhibit both high demand and offer high levels of response. Continued research, active listening and reflection will continually update leadership philosophies and responsiveness, as long as they resonate with core values.

Despite the busy days we experience, time for reflection is of vital importance, we need to give time for evaluating ourselves, to give focus and purpose to our leadership.

Context and distribution

Leadership begins with an understanding of the school community needs, aspirations and potential, demonstrating understanding of current values and those that can emerge and gain consensus over time.

True leadership is born through the determination of a vision, then developing the journey toward success, building clearly defined, mutual goals. The leader energizes the vision as it influences attitudes and empowers the enablers whilst also setting high expectations for performance. We also need to understand that quick fixes are a mirage. Success and continual uplifting of outcomes has its foundations in strategic, collaborative growth driven by focussed leadership. 'A highly effective school leader can have a dramatic influence on the overall academic achievement of students' (Fullan, 2005).

At the core of a successful school are empowered leaders at every level, because outstanding performance comes down to the motivation and actions of middle leaders and educators; a great school is no more than a series of great classrooms. Extending leadership capabilities into the classroom releases the latent talent and drive of teachers, creating powerful distributed leadership. Effective, optimistic leadership will always be the backbone of an effective school and is the core function of leadership to focus upon learning, teaching and people.

It is leadership that creates the vision and defines the strategic response that guides the school from vision to mission, building a shared vision and sense of purpose. In setting challenging goals our purpose is to inspire others to take risks, to express confidence and optimism, to encourage others to do more than they thought possible.

Great leaders perpetually manage change with the purpose of achieving the highest standards for all students through experiences, which offer them the opportunity to fully realise their potential as individuals. The best leaders ensure that improvement has direction; they create coherence through their vision, their passion, and the development of strong, effectively monitored structures. Beyond this it is all about sincerity, effort, and perspiration.

Each of us lead by example; we reward and foster excellence facilitating collaborative excellence as we strive to improve pedagogy and outcomes for every individual. The challenge is to provide autonomy to educators whilst simultaneously maintaining accountability, encouraging focused innovation informing pupils learning, and achievement. Fitzgerald, Gunter, Eaton (2006) concur that 'there can be little doubt that core imperative of educational leadership is student learning and student achievement' (p. 39). As others buy into vision and its purpose, leaders need to be constructive, ethical, open and honest.

These strategies support a culture of positive, engaging relationships; it is effective relationships that lie at the heart of effective learning and therefore an effective school. Engaging colleagues and distributing leadership and opportunity, entrusting responsibility to others is always essential as this process spreads the burden of leadership systematically. Entrusting responsibility to others also builds upon their individual strengths and resourcefulness. However in terms of ensuring sustainability and a common drive a balanced deployment of resources and control measures, focused upon agreed goals, must be ensured. Continually building upon the strengths of educators, sharing understanding and developing people is fundamental to success. Delegation and empowerment will support the growth of effective teams within the school as well as offering the opportunity to distribute leadership among the teams.

This approach will positively inform succession within the school which will both energise and develop leaders who are highly tuned to the philosophy of the school. Additionally, the role of the leader becomes one of role model, coach and facilitator as staff are empowered to act as leaders. We also need to develop new skills in our people, offering guidance, which will inform their growth and assure their success.

Leadership uniqueness and sustainability

Leadership styles form in a unique way over time reflecting the personal attributes, experience and knowledge of each individual. Each of us has experienced different leaders, different contexts and different sources of inspiration. Therefore, as no two individuals have experienced the same developmental pathway, our individual appreciation of leadership is context dependent; leadership style varies with personality and situational need.

It makes sense then that each of us must seek, develop and nurture our own vision, our own style, continually listening, learning, and adapting. Any vision must reflect the values and culture of the school providing a sense of purpose, built upon strong relationships, and working towards a common goal. Each of us must also consider that whilst each leadership style is exclusive to each individual, it is by no means static; it will grow through reflection and review, constantly being shaped unique contexts, environment, relationships, and experiences.

It is worth considering one of the greatest paradoxes of leadership; we strive to be authentic as we constantly drive for sustainability. Authentic leaders commit to the empowerment of others, developing both skills and opportunities to fuel sustainable change, developing a shared responsibility for the creation of an enhanced future for any school and professionals contained within.

The challenge lies in empowerment and informing a shared vision against the backdrop that each of us is a unique leader working in a unique environment. By engaging in constant dialogue with colleagues, listening, empathising and developing the individual skills for leadership succession, our intention is to create an environment in which sustainable leadership is fully embraced.

As leadership evolves, it is seeking to manage and lead an empowered workforce. Effective leaders are consultative and engaging, they empower yet are held to account when things go wrong.

There are many paradoxes we face day-to-day as we drive for inclusion and highly effective teams, yet individual praise and acknowledgement are vital. We empower staff yet have to be knowing and available to coach and mentor in order that we continually grow the potential of individuals within the school. At times, we will demonstrate authority yet we aspire to be collegiate and collaborative. We need to be safe and secure yet courageous in aligning our school's values and work purposefully toward defining and achieving the potential within our school. We take risks, define a compelling vision for our school and make it our mission to infuse within our colleagues a common sense of purpose and commitment as we drive toward a better future for our students.

Central to this authentic and courageous leadership is the development and communication of a compelling vision, motivating colleagues toward a commitment to that vision, always holding on to the notion that it is your vision that will sustain your courage as you move forward. Always bearing in mind that our first responsibility is to create a happy, stimulating, and challenging environment where students, staff and parents all have a significant role to play in building a happy, emotionally secure learning environment.

Well-being, engagement and happiness

The creation of a positive atmosphere is the joint responsibility of the professional and the parent communities. It starts at the top and requires an engaging proactive approach from all staff that is philosophically on the same page, focused by the schools vision statement and its pathway toward achieving its mission.

Everyone must understand that his or her contribution is essential and must be consistent in achieving a challenging and enjoyable atmosphere. We are always striving to achieve a situation where the students offer mutual respect to the teachers and the teachers enjoy working with and respect the students, where all concerned are comfortable with their 'happiness' contribution and the demands made of them. We all need to offer mutual respect and to enjoy and protect the 'well-being' of all; but sometimes we may just need to slow down, take the time to look and celebrate learning – even the simple act of sharing a smile will help.

The partnership of parents as role models is vital in reinforcing this appreciation of the efforts that both educators and students make on a daily basis. Parents are every student's first and life-long teacher; they are also vital as essential partners in developing, sustaining and nurturing affection for the community of any school.

A parent once shared with me: "Every day when I drop off my child at school, as I watch him walk towards the door, I wonder if the teachers truly understand that I am entrusting my most precious treasure to them." These are humbling words. As educators, we need to be aware of this trust, the importance of the responsibility we have and the incredible trust parents place in us. It reminds that the undisputed focus of every school, in every classroom and in everything we do is student learning, well-being and achievement.

Passion, an inspirational force

As leaders we must demonstrate that we are passionate in our beliefs, inspire those around us, build motivational forces and awaken staff to the possibilities of what they, their teams and the school can accomplish for our students. We must always talk the language of possibility. As leaders, it is essential that we articulate our vision, offer enthusiasm, and commitment to achieving our mission.

Passion is a powerful enabler, harnessing strong feelings, high levels of enthusiasm and devotion to a cause. Anyone driven by, and exhibiting, passion will infect those around them with their enthusiasm, converting and exciting others.

Trust and credibility are the currency of professional influence in this context. When you achieve high levels of mutual trust, engaged staff will want to help, inform and energise your vision. This model of investing in staff requires leaders who offer the ability to listen offering humility and passion. As a trusted channel we also strive for impact, we deal with high-performing teachers where a key function of leadership is to continually raise the bar and improve upon our existing levels of performance. In response, staff will feel empowered and encouraged and as objectives are met, deem that they themselves, with their teams, brought about improvements. Thus, a positive spiral of accomplishment will be generated.

As leaders, passionate about our schools and the journey we offer our students, we must continually display integrity, empathy, courage and confidence in a better tomorrow. Through our passion and commitment, we build mutual trust and respect through constant communication from professional presentations down to one-to-one coaching sessions.

Clearly conveying enthusiasm and selling the vision, successfully promoting a better future, and the strategic journey required to reach it, takes knowledge and passion. It is about transferring your own enthusiasm and belief to others, persuading them of the benefits for all concerned and the merits of the challenge. Only when staff truly understands and value potential outcomes for students and for themselves as teachers will they share in our vision.

This desired state can only be reached when senior leaders and mangers display a strong conviction for the mission, explaining in simple terms why it is preferable to the present state and adding vibrancy to the tasks ahead.

Communication is everything, but staff also needs to be confident that they can meet these needs; great leadership will constructively build ability and confidence, creating strong professional bonds and empathy.

Passion naturally carries empathy with it and is active, not passive. Lively presentation skills may come naturally but, for most leaders, calm restraint may be the norm, however, celebrating small successes to demonstrate progress will both impress and encourage. It is essential that the actions of leaders match their words whilst walking the talk actively demonstrates involved interest.

One-to-one and group coaching strengthens personal bonds, informing and calming those reluctant to take risks; great leaders always listen actively, the best listen with 'two ears and one mouth', listening twice as much as they talk. These behaviours subtly show and build commitment. Important rules apply: your team is always watching you; if you are feeling positive and confident, they will too, do not command, and do not demand too much, few have the same energy as leaders. In this way passion remains a positive force helping others understand the big picture, promoting collaboration, inclusive and requesting, offering promise, and drawing people in under the roof of one vision.

Leader as optimizer

An essential function of leadership is to optimize the performance and levels of engagement of students, parents and staff in order to inform student growth and achievement. As leaders, we must motivate and inspire new and challenging innovations encouraging educators to accomplish things that might seem beyond their grasp. At all times, no matter what the job throws at us we must portray a positive attitude about the ability of our teams to accomplish substantial things, to be successful. As academic leaders, we must provide intellectual stimulation, be active continual life-wide learners, sharing awareness, always encouraging others. Continually exposing staff to innovative ideas about how to be effective, encouraging professional debate about current theories and practices, constantly fuelling the fire of a strong academic culture, promoting continuous learning for all.

Great leaders are always self-effacing, self aware and willing to learn, they are always focused on student achievement, forever putting children's needs ahead of personal or political goals. They build sustainable structures and are purposeful and drive to build capacity in their schools. Most importantly they are willing to take risks, to challenge the status quo and to envision a better future for their students. They are excellent listeners, resilient and persistent but also adaptable and flexible; they are willing to seek, to understand, to work with and to motivate people toward a better future. When you get down to it, it's about making learning both enjoyable and challenging, developing schools which are flexible and responsive, as happy places to be. In the words of John Scully (2013): "The future belongs to those who see possibilities before they become obvious." That is where we make a difference ultimately involving everyone in a better future.

References and further reading

Al Maktoum, M. (2013) Flashes of Thought. Dubai: Motivate Publishing

Fullan M.(2005) *Leadership & sustainability: system thinkers in action.* Corwin Press

George, B. (2004) The journey to authenticity. *Leader to Leader*, No. 21. The Peter F. Drucker Foundation for Nonprofit Management

Cialdini, R. B. (2006) *Influence: The Psychology of Persuasion.* Boston, MA: Allyn and Bacon

Fitzgerald, T. & Gunter, H. with Eaton, J. (2006) The missing link?: Middle leadership in schools in New Zealand and England. *New Zealand Journal of Educational Leadership*, 29-43

Scully, J (2013) *Famous quotes at Brainy Quote.* [online] Brainy Quote. Available at http// brainyquote.com. [Accessed 7 May 2014]

Chapter 6

Wellbeing: a predictor of success

'Each morning when I open my eyes I say to myself: I, not events, have the power to make me happy or unhappy today. I can choose which it shall be. Yesterday is dead, tomorrow hasn't arrived yet. I have just one day, today, and I'm going to be happy in it.' (Groucho Marx)

As we face the challenges of rapid change and developing strategies for learning in the 21st century we must never lose sight of the fact that people matter. They can inform the future success of any school, their well-being and engagement are essential if a school is to develop or improve its performance. The future requires that the well being of the whole staff is nurtured as an energizer for change. As leaders we must focus upon change that will bring about positive outcomes, we have power to influence those around us and in return be influenced ourselves; we live with a purpose and in that context well being matters.

The concept of well-being comprises feeling good and functioning well. Feelings of happiness, contentment, enjoyment, curiosity and engagement are characteristic of individuals who have a positive outlook on life. Equally important for well-being is our sense of purpose and place, our function in the world. Experiencing positive relationships, having some control over one's life and having a sense of purpose are all important attributes of well-being. However, well-being is not an outcome; it is something which broadens our perspective, a predictor of future success.

We all want to be happy

The state of well-being and satisfaction largely depends upon the thinking of an individual, yet the quest for well-being, for happiness, is universal; everyone wants to be happy. I think we would all agree that well-being and happiness put us on the road to fulfillment accepting that happiness is a journey, not a destination. We must acknowledge how complex it is as it is always influenced by traits such as optimism, gratitude, zest, curiosity, and love regardless of age or financial context.

All these traits can be nurtured and encouraged; there are many routes to happiness. The word happy is an emotionally positive word, it offers a positive message, opening dialogue and always a driver that helps us drive to make a better world. Yet we need to understand this, is happiness a trait, 'I am a happy person', or a state, 'I am happy today'. Happiness is complex: is it an emotion, a reflection of people lives? We all need to understand what makes us happy and our accounts of well-being.

Considering happiness gives us a momentum for change where knowledge and engagement become empowering tools, even discussing happiness is a win-win

Every school is unique and special and as leaders we must always be open and honest, paying attention to and being mindful of the well being of our community. Mindful leaders are self-aware, ethical, clear-sighted and relationally transparent. They are trusted and they are effective and they create the environment for great learning.

Professional development to support teacher well-being has become an emergent theme, one which supports better and more secure learning. Positive, optimistic, happy people are mentally, physically, and emotionally healthier more able to access new learning. They are more resilient, have better relationships, are more successful at work and are satisfied with their lives and careers. Research suggests they even live longer!

Being mindful will always have a positive impact upon well-being (Huppert & Johnson 2010). Well-being makes us feel good and if we feel good we can display happiness, contentment interest and affection. The positivity of well-being encourages in each of us the ability to make choices and offers resilience in the face of challenges, enhances curiosity and creativity.

The positive impact of well-being

In recent years there has been a growing acceptance that the well-being of a school community has a positive impact upon the formal outcomes of school activity. It directly informs student capacity for learning and achievement.

As leaders we must understand how we are perceived on a day-to-day basis and the impact we have on our educators. The very designation of Headteacher is an impediment, accepting that we must always demonstrate awareness and be proactive in considering and bring a steady focus upon staff well being. As leaders we need to have a progressive and empowering mindset in order that we foster positivity and understand the expectations of our talented staff.

The best thing for any school is an engaged, happy and motivated staff who know they are valued by their leaders. As leaders we must aspire to create a context which allows, indeed encourages our staff to flourish. Flourishing creates a positive effect. According to Fredrickson and Losada (2005), to flourish means to live with an optimal range of human functioning: one that connotes goodness, growth and resilience. Keyes (2002) argues that people can move from languishing to flourishing and function well if they develop positive emotional wellbeing, positive social well-being and positive psychological well-being.

We may be lucky enough to have teachers who display high levels of social and emotional competence; it is likely that we model and nurture these attributes, but do we need to create the opportunity to provide explicit training in the development of skills such as compassion, gratitude and empathy? I would not underestimate either the value or the challenge of such development, as developing social and emotional skills in adults is a complex process.

For our teachers, these skills are imperative not only for their personal well-being but to improve student learning.

Teacher well-being is relevant

The best thing for students is a happy, motivated staff. Teacher well-being is relevant for whole school well-being, informing a stable, secure social and learning environment for students.

Murray-Harvey (2010) found that both academic outcomes and social and emotional well-being in school were 'unambiguously influenced' by the quality of relationships between teachers and students. By putting the motivation and engagement of staff alongside the students, you are doing the best you can do for the students. Yes we put the needs of the students first but they are far from our sole responsibility. If we do not pay attention to our educators and support staff we are doing our learners a disservice.

When teachers are at ease with their responsibilities, when they have a sense of professional autonomy they project that same sense of wellbeing into their learning environments making learning an enjoyable act, a goal to which all of us are dedicated. We must access the creativity and potential within our teaching teams supporting and encouraging our talented teachers to both inform and thrive in positive, collaborative environments.

The outcomes include positive effects for children's knowledge and attainment, and also teachers' professional commitment, knowledge and satisfaction. (Goddard *et al*, 2004).

The work goes on to outline seven pathways to well-being in a school:

- Building a respectful and supportive school community.
- Developing pro-social values.
- Providing a safe learning environment.
- Enhancing social-emotional learning.
- Using strengths based approaches.
- Fostering a sense of meaning and purpose.
- Encouraging a healthy lifestyle.

Listening

We all know people who are really good listeners. No matter what the context they always know what to say, how and when to say it. They offer a high level of care and consideration, they are active listeners able to put aside their own viewpoint trying to see things from another's perspective. Not only do they listen with their ears, they listen with their eyes and their heart as they considers not only what is being said, but what the other person feels.

Active listening brings the focus of attention to the speaker and what they have to say, a way of listening and responding to another person that promotes mutual understanding. Leaders who have a high degree of emotional intelligence are effective listeners; they are capable of offering positive solutions without causing offence or upset. They are caring, considerate and others usually leave feeling valued, motivated, and optimistic.

This mindful listening is deeply powerful, it involves listening with integrity and honesty and responding with compassion and understanding. Mindful listening offers kindness and insight to both colleagues and students in times of need and is critical to mutually supportive relationships.

A smile is a charity

A smile is a universal means of communicating, it's also one of the most basic expressions of all, smiles are cross-cultural and have the same meaning in different societies. More than 30% of us smile more than 20 times a day. Some, less than 14% of us, smile less than five times a day. In fact one of the reasons schools are such great places to work is that children smile as many as 400 times daily, great for us as educators as our natural reflex is to return a smile, it's contagious and happiness is activated when we smile.

The brain, in seeing a smile, has already considered the reward attained. More often we need to access the power of authentic smiles, according to Gutman (2011) it has the ability to connect us with others, we will be happier and healthier.

"Too often, we underestimate the power of a touch, a smile, a kind word, a listening ear, an honest compliment, or the smallest act of caring, all of which have the potential to turn a life around" (Leo F. Buscaglia, 1994).

Recognition, acknowledgement and unexpected kindness

Recognition is hugely important: just two hours a week in acts of unexpected kindness will inform an emotionally literate school. A school where leaders find teachers doing great things, have the time to listen to, to prompt, encourage and demonstrate care for their teachers and give positive feedback for their efforts will inform great learning for students. Therefore you must seek out colleagues, catch them doing great things and tell them why and how well they are doing.

We all like praise. I know I need to tell people more often how much I appreciate them, but I keep trying, I can never do enough.

Something special is happening here

We all feel good when someone thanks us. Our purpose should always focus upon the special things that happen in our schools. Recognising that 'something special is happening here', is highly rewarding and motivating for all concerned. We need to build the happy gene!

Key to effective leadership is to maintain and develop positivity and high morale; we need to be systematic and fair in recognising, celebrating and sharing the accomplishments of our students and teachers. Recognition supports motivation across any school, fuelling high performance and reinforcing desired behaviours, building a culture of high performance and high levels of motivation. As leaders we need to utilise and value recognition, acknowledging that whether recognition works for us is not the point: it works for others.

Simply recognizing the effort staff commit to their work will raise levels of motivation and morale. My point here is that recognition is a leadership tool; the work of Robert Cialdani (2006) identifies recognition as an effective device that can be used to lead and motivate people other than you. You never know, someone may just come along and acknowledge you someday. Ultimately, you have to admit that it is good for you, it is good for your school, and it is the right thing to do.

Our parents were right all along, it's just polite to say "thank you" and is a great way to build relationship capital, or to create a reciprocity pool.

In saying recognition is the right thing to do, it must be deserved and our response to excellence must be authentic, not automatic. You have to mean it. When we apply recognition, we have a positive impact upon areas such as engagement, attendance, collaboration, retention and most importantly learning and teaching. We need to make time to get into our classrooms, catch people doing exemplary work, sharing great experiences. We then need to thank them and tell them how they are doing such a great job. Our professional colleagues merit constructive feedback and positive affirmation or simply saying, "thank you" for a job well done.

Recognising the great things happening around you in your school will make it a happier place to be, for everyone. Put simply: it feels great to work in an organisation where morale is high!

Being mindful is an inherent human capacity. But it doesn't always come naturally, it requires discipline and practice to focus on the 'here and now' and not get sidetracked by past mistakes or future results. Mindful leaders are able to achieve this; they are less concerned about individual success and self-esteem issues, and are better able to form deeper meaningful connections and relationships with those they lead.

We are all mindful to one degree or another, moment by moment. Effective leaders are attentive, aware of and value the opinions of colleagues and their experiences, engaging in conversations that cross the boundaries of function and hierarchy, this way they gain new perspectives from as well as trust and deeper engagement from staff.

Promoting positive well-being amongst colleagues makes a huge difference. When staff feel appreciated and empowered, they are willing to share their practice and demonstrate greater empathy for the learners in their care. This enhances the capacity of any school to nurture and developing students' potential. Children with higher levels of emotional, behavioural, social, and school wellbeing, on average, have higher levels of academic achievement.

Student well-being

As leaders we must acknowledge the difference we can make by embracing the notion of student well being within and beyond the academic context.

We need to foster well-being because there is a link between well-being, academic and personal success. Implicit modeling of well-being may already be the source of positive engagement with our students but we have to consider whether or not we can be deliberate, explicit in our approach and target the well-being domains.

We should following the example of Geelong Grammar School, who have actively implemented a Positive Education program in recent years. In a school-wide context they target six well-being domains, including positive emotions, positive engagement, positive accomplishment, positive purpose, positive relationships, and positive health, underpinned by a focus on character strengths (Norrish *et al,* 2013).

Positive Education is essentially traditional education focused on academic skill development complemented by approaches that nurture well-being and promote good mental health (Seligman, 2011). The program aims to increase mental fitness and resilience for every student who in the best of circumstances has a personal tutor who identifies strengths and sets overseas academic and personal goals. Students are also introduced to activities which are scientifically proven to increase levels of well-being and performance.

Positive Education could more completely be described as bringing together the science of Positive Psychology with best-practice teaching to encourage students to flourish. Students flourishing is simply viewed as both 'feeling good' and 'doing good' (Huppert & So, 2013). Feeling good reflects a wide range of emotions and experiences such as happiness with the present and hopeful for the future. Doing good strives to equip students with capability to help them to face both the challenges and opportunities which life offers. A focus on well-being within education is beneficial and supports student achievement. Howell (2009) found that students who were flourishing reported superior grades, higher self-control and positive attendance rates.

Creating a culture of well-being will develop a positive approach where members of the school community see great purpose in their life, their work and the goals of the school as well as greater self-awareness. It will engender more meaningful and satisfying learning and personal relationships enhancing both student and teacher capability, resilience and their potential to cope with the demands of school life.

Positive interventions from leaders increase wellbeing, enhancing engagement and a perception of value from the school, its purpose and its vision. It will also encourage positive relations with others, personal growth and role purpose.

Being positive will inform success.

According to Fredrickson (2001), positive emotions broaden our thoughts and actions: we pay more attention, are more creative, flexible and are open to relationships. Positive emotions build psychological resources: resilience, coping, physical abilities, emotional intelligence, social skills and self mastery. Taking this into consideration these attributes will inform positive outcomes and it's reasonable to say that the only true disability in life is a negative attitude, life may not appear to be fair at times but it has a habit of responding to a positive attitude.

Life is your attitude, and we should have attitude with gratitude. Consider the great things you have, the great things within you and the unlimited potential of your future as well as the positive impact you can have on those around you.

A final consideration: 'Educating the mind without educating the heart is no education at all' – Aristotle.

References and further reading

Buscaglia L.F. (1994) Born for Love: *Reflections on Loving*. Fawcett Columbine

Cialdini, R. B. (2006): *Influence: The psychology of Persuasion*

Fredrickson B. (2001) The role of positive emotions in positive psychology: The broaden-and-build theory of positive emotions. *American psychologist.* 56 (3), p218–226

Fredrickson, B. (2009). *Positivity*. London: Crown Publishers

Fredrickson, B., Losada, M. (2005) Positive Affect and the Complex Dynamics of Human Flourishing: *American Psychologist*, Vol 60

Goddard, R. D., Hoy, W. K. & Woolfolk, H. A. (2004). Collective efficacy beliefs: Theoretical developments, empirical evidence and future directions. *Educational Researcher*, 33(3), p. 3–13

Gutman, R. (2011) *Smile: The Astonishing Powers of a Simple Act*. New York: Ted Books

Howell, A. J. (2009). Flourishing: Achievement-related correlates of students' well-being. *Journal of Positive Psychology*, 4(1), p. 1-13. http://dx.doi.org/10.1080/17439760802043459

Huppert, F. A., & So, T. T. (2013). Flourishing across Europe: Application of a new conceptual framework for defining well-being. *Social Indicators Research*, 110(3), p. 837-861

Murray-Harvey, R. (2010). Relationship influences on students' academic achievement, psychological health and well-being at school. *Educational and Child Psychology*, 27(1), 104–113

Norrish, J. M., Williams, P., O'Connor, M., & Robinson, J. (2013). An applied framework for positive education. *International Journal of Wellbeing*, 3(2), 147-161

Seligman, M. (2011). *Flourish*. London: Nicholas Brealey Publishing

Chapter 7

Positive mindsets, positive learners

If we are to truly embrace learning and the intellectual growth of our students then we need to understand that intelligence can be incrementally grown and the role of effort in nurturing and creating talent. In order to develop a growth mindset for our students we must carefully maintain in all of our students confidence and effectiveness in the face of the challenges we offer and the inevitable setbacks experienced. The four beliefs and the four truths (Dweck, 2000) about the positive impact of nurturing ability, identifying and rewarding success, considered and well- focused praise as well as maintaining and growing individual confidence will be at the heart of our considerations. Having talent is just a starting point.

It has been said that success is down 10% to natural ability and 90% to hard work. However, individual effort needs to be clearly focussed upon personal growth and the development of new skills.

The basketball player Michael Jordan is a good case in point. He is often viewed as a 'natural' but, in his early days Jordan did not show a great deal of promise but he persevered, trained harder than anyone else and paid attention to and focused effort upon developing his weaknesses.

Intelligence is a physical process

Intelligence is a physical process that resists confinement, it is a skill that we can all exercise and improve. It's about having a having a positive approach to learning and growing to become better than you thought you could ever be. We are not born intelligent; as babies we learn continually. Rarely do you see unmotivated babies; they are all highly engaged learners. That said, you may witness unmotivated adults.

Scientists have been able to show just how the brain grows and gets stronger when you learn, much like a muscle; it changes and gets stronger when you use it. When each of our students truly believes in their developing abilities, they will thrive. How can that not be true? We, as educators can be the catalysts, but ultimately everything is within our students' control. Their intelligence can be influenced; it can be shaped and formed incrementally, over time. Our primary function is to teach them that they can grow their potential and that they are in charge of their intellectual growth.

Positive mindsets

The belief that intelligence can be developed will open in our students a deep love of learning. This positive mindset can determine how we think, our actions and what outcomes we achieve in life. It is our singularly unique mind that holds the key to real success for all of us. Of course, each individual has a unique genetic endowment; we all start with different aptitudes and temperaments. Beyond these initial gifts it is clear that personal experience, effort, education and training inform our unique journey through life, not just school. Ultimately the answer lies in the ongoing experiences that develop and create all of us.

Successful individuals are mastery-oriented:

- They love learning;
- They seek challenges;
- They value effort; and
- They persist in the face of obstacles.

People with a growth mindset have a completely different view of success and failure. Of course, we are all motivated by success and want to achieve it, but for them success as a result of being stretched and knowing that you have mastered something is hugely rewarding. Learning new skills isn't seen as an acknowledgement of intelligence or talent, it is viewed as a reward for effort and commitment. When things become difficult, or even when they go wrong, these positive learning attributes focus upon the view of failure not as a negative, but as something they can learn from to inform future success.

Within our schools we need to accept the principle that great people and great minds are made, not born and outstanding, continual learners learn to fail intelligently. Recently scientists have learned that people have more capacity for life-long learning and brain development than they ever thought, and it's not always the people who start out the smartest who end up the smartest.

Yet this is not a new phenomena. Thomas Edison when striving toward the discovery of a functioning light bulb is credited with saying, "If I find 10,000 ways something won't work, I haven't failed. I am not discouraged, because every wrong attempt discarded is another step forward." Clearly a bright man!

We should praise children for qualities they can control, like effort. Those praised for their innate brainpower might develop the sense that hard work isn't necessary.

In life, in learning, any meaningful success requires effort. When we focus praise upon effort instead of intelligence we can further motivate, inspire and develop every student within our schools. However we need to be aware that when children are praised for how intelligent they are, they become focused on retaining this label rather than on continuing to learn.

Dweck argues praise for intelligence may seem a positive thing to do but can distort children's attitude to learning as they become more interested in how they are seen by others than in the learning itself. We would all acknowledge the value of praise as very important for children's performance and confidence; praise can ignite that innate desire to achieve.

The key question here is what should we praise? Research promotes praise of persistence despite difficulties, application of new strategies, good choices and selection of difficult tasks. Learning itself and striving for improvement also merit praise, but most importantly we should praise effort, because effort is required for success in all areas of endeavour.

Ability can change

Once we acknowledge that ability can change we can then begin to create a growth mindset in every student. As educators we can demonstrate ourselves as incremental learners and effective role models it is essential that we show them we believe their intelligence is not fixed. We need to make them believe they can improve as well as ensuring that they know how to improve.

The development of our classrooms as environments of possibility, collaborative learning environment where pupils take responsibility for their own learning, and students with a growth mindset see effort as a necessary part of success. Our students will then try harder when faced with a setback and use effort to overcome difficulty, adopting a positive mindset capable of generating other, new and better ways to do things. They will think 'outside of the box' to solve problems because they believe that they can. This will encourage in all students a willingness to be more open to learning, willing to confront challenges, able to stick at difficult tasks and capable of bouncing back from failures.

Great feedback is essential

To further support these positive learning environments great feedback is essential, a key influence on student learning as supported by John Hattie's (2008) research:

	Effect Size
Feedback	0.73
Teacher-Student Relationships	0.72
Mastery Learning	0.58
Challenge of Goals	0.56
Peer Tutoring	0.55
Expectations	0.43
Homework	0.29
Aims & Policies of the School	0.24
Ability Grouping	0.12

His research clearly denotes the importance of feedback in enhancing student performance. However, if feedback is so important, what kind of feedback should be taking place in our classrooms?

Constructive criticism is will always be a key feature, necessary if we want students to develop and learn. Praise for the effort and the process will help our students become more motivated and ultimately more resilient. Students will do anything for teachers they like and trust.

Love of learning and value for effort

As educators we can actively support a culture of a growth mindset our students have a greater possibility of becoming successful individuals who will on a daily basis demonstrate a love of learning, value for effort and the ability to persist in the face of obstacles. In order to further support them we are required to intentionally choose words and actions that are optimistic, respectful, trustworthy and caring. We just need to see them as able, valuable and responsible capable of making responsible choices. Critically we need to demonstrate awareness of and respect for their unique individuality, talent and potential with high expectations for all students in all ability groupings.

If we are honest with students about where they are and what they need to do to improve, if we have the courage and the good sense to promote a positive view of errors and mistakes in the classroom praise wisely and reward effort we will do much to create so much potential in so many students in a happy active and engaging learning context.

As educators we should always demonstrate a constant desire to learn and improve, constantly promoting inquiry, communication and reflection in a collaborative environment to the benefit of every young adult in our care, as we will develop potential and skills which will support them on their life-long learning journey.

References and further reading

Dweck, C. S. (2007) *Mindset: The New Psychology of Success.* Ballentine Books

Dweck C. (2000) *Self-theories: Their Role in Motivation, Personality, and Development:* Psychology Press, 2000

Hattie, J. (2008) *Visible Learning: A Synthesis of Over 800 Meta-Analyses Relating to Achievement.* Routledge: New York

Hattie, J. (2011) *Visible Learning for Teachers: Maximizing Impact on Learning.* Routledge: New York

Chapter 8

Why do we think of a building when we talk about learning?

We now live in a 'learn anything, anywhere, anytime' world. Last century people believed that you were born with what you got and that was that! We also know that intelligence is not fixed; you cannot put a ceiling on what any individual can be expected to achieve. As educators we are moulding the intellectual capacity of the future of the world, our true test is to develop in young people the appetite for knowledge and the capacity to learn. To this end our aim is to develop curious, passionate, creative, and better equipped life-long learners.

Accepting Da Vinci's claim that, 'the desire to know is natural to good men', we must offer each and every student the opportunity to grow and time to think about what and how they are learning. Our focus is not just our teaching it is also on helping our students become better learners offering access to multiple styles an approaches as no learning style is 'better'

How did we get here?
Throughout the 18th and 19th Centuries, education developed around the notion of supporting the development of the industrial revolution, retraining students coming from an agrarian economy and instilling discipline, punctuality, concentration and the ability to

receive information, learning was a process of acquiring. Education was separated into small testable bits and then assessed. Today we are facing changes regarding how we learn, what we learn and where we learn. The journey our young learners are travelling will not allow us to teach them all they need to know because we cannot with certainty determine what that future will be.

> In times of change, learners inherit the Earth, while the learned find themselves beautifully equipped to deal with a world that no longer exists. (Eric Hoffer, 1902-83)

We are in danger of not seeing the wood for the trees; our national curriculum has been developed into a small forest of clearly defined subjects, when we should be focusing upon the needs of each individual, building their learning potential, building the brain. Defining education, like life itself, as a process of becoming.

Learning is an evolutionary, learnable skill

Recognising that learning is an evolutionary, learnable skill, we need to be committed to the creation of powerful and confident, life-long learners. As educators our primary responsibility is to facilitate children's learning, developing flexible, creative thinkers, giving them the skills to deal with and respond positively to the complexities of life. We need to give our learners the confidence to begin to take responsibility for their own learning, exploring their own lines of enquiry, learning from peers and adults the distinctions between teacher and learner will narrow.

This will demand considerable agility from all in terms of the learning-centered roles required whether it be teacher, expert, facilitator, learner, mentor or coach. When we are faced with a new challenge in life, we do what humans do best: we learn, adapt and develop a strategy for dealing with the challenge. Today's rapid pace of change means that we have to continue to develop throughout our lives in order to survive, to keep pace with challenges of the 21st century. Consequently every school must simultaneously close the gap and raise the bar.

Each of us has the capacity and ability to learn. Children will take a chance, if they don't know, they will have a go. They are not frightened of being wrong, if you're not prepared to be wrong you'll never come up with anything original; in the words of Wayne Gresky, "you miss 100% of the shots you don't take". Being frightened of being wrong is one of the concerning challenges of our education system; I prefer to take the view that the only real failure in life is the failure to try. Our brains are physically moulded by our experiences, and "success is the ability to go from one failure to another with no loss of enthusiasm" (Winston Churchill).

Mistakes and points of stuckness are key points in the exploration of learning. When we create contexts where our students focused on their learning failure has the potential to instil challenge and continued effort as opposed to a dependency response.

Cells that fire together wire together
Accepting that there can be a two-to-three-year spread in neurological maturation between students with the same birthday we must always be careful about labelling and defining students' capabilities. Our job is not only to fully realise the potential of our students but also to increase that potential. A 21st Century view is cells that fire together wire together. The process of learning is actually about making, then strengthening new connections in the brain over time: cells that fire together wire together.

We need to be careful as if we do not re-fire new connections within an hour or so we lose them, forgetting 80% within 24 hours (Ebbinghaus Curve of Forgetting, 1885). A review of learning is imperative at the end of lessons, and then at the onset of future lessons after a day, a week, a month, or even a year. It can promote a 400% improvement in memory. Review of learning is not an optional extra.

We can grow our brain
The brain is dynamic, it grows as we learn. Learning changes the physical structure of the brain adding synapses, learning literally involves re-wiring the brain. With positive dynamics such as commitment, curiosity, positive attitude, effort and communication we can develop new skills continually enhancing performance. Essentially, the functions of the brain can be strengthened just like a weak muscle; it can grow, and will, with practice! The more we learn the more connections we make, the more we use it, the more we can use it as we, 'seek out challenging experiences that develop their skills and knowledge' (Dweck 2000).

The brain is like a muscle and needs to be worked to develop in a healthy way, it has to be used in order for it to grow. Your brain needs to be cared for, like any muscle: when depleted, it becomes less effective. Furthermore, we should take this knowledge into account when making decisions. Correct nutrition, sleep, lack of stress is more important than design of learning. We have to be ready to learn. Sleep helps the mind learn complicated tasks and helps people recover learning they otherwise thought they had forgotten over the course of a day, research at the University of Chicago shows (Nusbaum *et al*, 2008). Sleep has an important role in learning generalized skills in stabilizing and protecting memory.

Looking ahead we need a better balance if we are to be truly learner centered, a greater focus upon skills, higher order thinking, life skills and learning for life. We need enhance learning opportunities and learning skills to support innovation and develop critical thinking skills. We need to develop in them the courage to accept new challenges, courage to engage with uncertain things, to risk, to see what happens 'to boldly go'. We need to develop in our learners the ability to change and the desire for life-long learning, the determination to stick with things that are difficult, to be patient, persistent and robust learners, able to pick themselves up, dust themselves down and get the job done.

To be ready to learn, our young people need curiosity; curiosity is a starting point for learning, if you are interested in things, you will engage. Curiosity encourages students to wonder about things: how they come to be, and how they work. Develop curiosity in students and you will stimulate questioning, investigation, discussion, thought. Effective learning is supported by purposeful collaboration and participation with a curriculum which is both active and learner focused.

Effective learners know who to talk to and when to talk about their learning. They are good team members, know how to listen, how to take turns and offer helpful contributions. Effective learners stay open-minded to and respectful of others' views; collective learning is important to them. They are generous in sharing information, ideas and useful ways of thinking and exploring; and they are willing to accept alternative perspectives (Claxton, 2002). Exploration is the active, inquisitive counterpart of curiosity, and we learn from experimenting and from being inquisitive. Our learners need to be skilled at seeking and gathering information, enjoying the process of finding things out, of researching and reading.

What are we learning?

In the last century information was power and experts knew all the answers. The key learning skill, the key measurable, was our ability to remember stuff! Today information is like water, you can turn it on and turn it off and it is easily accessible to all. However we need to be careful because it has a limited shelf life. The key skill today is embracing change, because things change so fast. It is estimated that things change in the business world four times faster than within education; are we to continue to fall behind?

This rapid pace of change means that, "the illiterate of the 21st Century are not those who cannot read or write, but those who cannot learn unlearn, and relearn" (Alvin Toffler, 1972).

There is so much more to education than learning and regurgitating facts. The mile wide and inch deep approach where the single purpose of education is passing a test rather than an actively engaged enquirer is simply inadequate for young people in the 21st century. Of course there are facts, core concepts and knowledge that we need to have at our fingertips but our students aspire to thrive in dynamic and engaging classrooms which value them as learners and people with a part to play and something to say. Educators and politicians alike have long debated the value of learning the basics or critical thinking skills.

The truth is our students' need both to effectively engage in the 21st Century; it is in the knowing and application of learning and new knowledge where truly authentic education emerges. As educators we create the future today through our actions and the purposeful nature of our work.

Teaching is inherently agile and educators can more often maximize their classroom potential in an environment in which they are trusted and have the professional capability to be flexible and adaptive, offering a range of teaching approaches. They are motivated by the drive to inspire learning, to nurture curiosity and creativity for their students. In order to grow the individual potential of every student we need to see learning through their eyes; to encourage them to learn in depth we need to be deliberate in building upon their previous learning and constantly stretch them beyond their comfort zones.

Developing deep learning

In focusing on the learning process we are rephrasing the learning partnerships between and among students and teachers, developing students' ability to take responsibility for and even lead their own learning. We need to develop opportunities for deep learning which goes beyond the mastery of content knowledge, instead encouraging human inquiry, creativity, and purposeful learning. To that end we need to foster collaborative and communicative learning environments which offer learning outcomes not only focused upon literacy and numeracy but also acknowledge outcomes such as problem-solving, creativity, critical thinking, collaboration and teamwork skills.

Digital media and technology, effectively integrated, can change pedagogy and the learning paradigm. They offer new contexts for learning informing opportunities for rapid, accessible and empowered learning. Mobile learning devices are powerful, personal and highly accessible; they are already integrated into life and continual learning. That said, these are only tools to support learning and must be approached as such, like a pair of scissors, available as required and put aside when not; a tool for empowerment.

As both leaders and educators we need to consider and be proactive in developing opportunities for pedagogical growth, curriculum enhancement and empowered learning. Ultimately we can encourage and nurture a culture which values risk taking and ensure that our students are challenged intellectually at an appropriate level.

Connect to previous learning

When teachers connect student learning to previous learning and other settings they offer the opportunity for students to think flexibly applying their knowledge and thinking more deeply as they contribute and express their own ideas and experiences in a new learning context. With the teacher acting in what is often referred to as a facilitative mode, I prefer to use the term activator (Fullan 2013). As teachers engage in learning alongside students, actively participating, the learning process becomes one of mutual discovery, creation and sharing. Teachers need to be both aware and measured in this learning paradigm, not too directive, nor passive, a fine balance always based upon great learning relationships and active engagement with learners, where learning is reciprocal and in the best of situations, mutually beneficial.

In this context educators can see learning through the eyes of their students; they build trusting relationships and are simultaneously challenging students to reach for the next level in their learning.

Getting the right kind of feedback is essential to promote learning

Carol Dweck's research has shown that the 'right kind' of feedback is that which encourages taking on hard challenges and focuses on students' efforts rather than their achievements. In this context there is great potential for effective feedback as it can be offered within the learning process and this is highly effective. However it will demand that the teacher is both adaptable and flexible responding to student progress in 'the moment'.

Another key element is that feedback is focused upon helping students to understand their work more clearly in relation to agreed learning goals (Wiliam, 2010). These strategies will continually build students' awareness of the process of learning, a goal in itself, and help teachers understand which teaching and learning strategies best activate an individual student's learning

Teach them how to listen

Understanding that effective listening is both rare and valuable, as well as being essential to the learning process, we need to teach our students how to listen. When we listen effectively we engage with our peers, make eye contact, offer empathy and resist the temptation to cut in. Good listeners are often well-liked and these attributes can inform an engaging learning situation with good listeners demonstrating patience, deliberate thinking and in the best of cases confirming shared ideas which indicate the next step in their collaboration.

To create these highly collaborative, student-centered classrooms as teachers we need to model listening, measured questioning and negotiated learning at every opportunity, after all learning is a social process (Vygotsky, 1978).

Deeper learning can improve student outcomes

The demands of a fast changing, global economy requires students with high levels of literacy, students who are technologically adept with the capacity to innovate and to think critically. Schools can support such students by creating dynamic learning environments that enable students to develop a deep understanding of core knowledge, skills and content which they can then apply in communicating, solving problems, critical thinking and reflection.

Deeper learning is the ability to transfer previously acquired knowledge and skills to new contexts, an inspirational goal for any learner. Deeper learning is simply what highly effective educators offer every day: the delivery of rich and coherent curriculum which focuses upon the students as learners and their potential to solve real-life problems which will stretch, challenge and engage young minds. They apply an innovative pedagogy to allow students to apply learning and previous knowledge to new contexts. A clear and driven focus upon learning in core subjects is an enabler for deep learning.

Deeper learning prepares students to:

- know and demonstrate mastery of core knowledge and skills.
- know how to use that knowledge to think critically and solve problems.
- engage in collaborative work, communicating their thinking using a variety of media.
- learn how to learn and to be reflective.

In this context, teaching shifts from delivery of required content to a focusing on the learning process, developing students' ability to lead their own learning and to do things with their learning. Teachers are partners with students in deep learning tasks characterised by exploration, connectedness and broader, real-world purposes.

The emergence of a community of practice

As outlined by Michael Fullan (2010), learning outcomes can be measured in terms of students capacities to build new knowledge and to lead their own learning effectively, learning which has a strong element of real life problem-solving. The nature of learning relationships between students and teachers are changing, so much more is expected of our students today and they need our expertise, challenge and support in order to build and maintain their confidence through feedback and encouragement. Our aim must always be one of continually acknowledging and building upon their success and culturing within them a positive awareness of their own potential. Ultimately, these pedagogies foster a new kind of learning that is more purposeful, engaging and connected to real life.

A learner-centered school will focus upon the need to continue to support the emergence of community of practice developed through teamwork, collaboration and sharing, defining a school where learning is focused upon the needs and interests of the learner and owned by the learner. We need to encourage the development of personal skills, the development of personality, the talents and abilities of our young people to the full.

How do you develop in students the ability to be courageous, inquisitive, or sociable? We need to develop a language for learning, trust young people more and offer support, opportunity and challenge to them. Crucially, the school and all the adults in it need to continually model the virtues of life-long learning in their own professional lives. Schools need to develop intentional learners who can adapt to new environments, integrate knowledge from different sources, and continue learning throughout their lives. Intentional learners are empowered, informed and responsible (Greater Expectations 2002 AACU Report).

Becoming an intentional learner means developing self-awareness about the reason for study and how to integrate knowledge, to see connections in learning which informs their thinking. Being self-directed, these learners are highly motivated and independent, striving for autonomy. They take the initiative for their learning, formulate learning goals, identify resources for learning and select and implement learning strategies.

Today the winds are changing, everyone can create and contribute, and everyone is an expert! Being able to think carefully, rigorously and methodically, as well as to take an imaginative leap, the ability to follow a rigorous train of thought are invaluable skills. We need to learn how to learn, to continually adapt and grow, to know what to know and learn what to learn but finding the good stuff is hard. Information literacy is an understanding and of abilities which enable individuals to 'recognise when information is needed and have the capacity to locate, evaluate, and use effectively the required information'.

Educators who deliberately activate learning

Teachers must always begin with the end in mind. Effective learning must be authentic applying skills and knowledge to real world problems and challenges. It must be rigorous promoting and measuring learning against learning standards with educators deliberatively activating learning, applying an appropriate level of intervention to enable students to understand their success and to develop their competencies.

Teachers will often serve as coaches and facilitators of inquiry and reflection in this context, they will also be able to take advantage of multiple opportunities to feedback to students encouraging them to reflect and revise their work. This more dynamic approach to learning is allowing students to explore real world problems and challenges. As active and engaged learners, students have the opportunity to gain deeper knowledge of their work as they learn through questioning, inquiry, and critical thinking.

According to researchers (Barron & Darling-Hammond, 2008) students learn effectively when they tackle realistic problems, when they engage in inquiry, real world problems. Inquiry based teaching methods engage students in creating, questioning, and revising knowledge, while developing their skills in critical thinking, collaboration and communication. Above all students can take control of their learning, developing positive attitudes toward their work as it more often aligns with their aptitudes and interests.

References and further reading

Barell, J. (2007) *Problem-Based Learning: An Inquiry Approach.* Thousand Oaks: Corwin Press

Barron, B., & Darling-Hammond, L. (2008). *Powerful Learning: What We Know About Teaching for Understanding.* San Francisco, CA: Jossey-Bass

Brawn, T., Fenn, K., Nusbaum, H., et al. (2008) *Consolidation of sensorimotor learning during sleep.* Cold Spring Harbor Laboratory Press

Claxton, C. (2002) *Building Learning Power: Helping Young People Become Better Learners.* Bristol: TLO

Dweck, C. (2000). *Self-Theories: Their role in motivation, personality and development. Essays in social psychology.* Philadelphia, PA: Psychology Press

Dweck, C. (2005). 'How Can Teachers Develop Students' Motivation - and Success?' Interview by Gary Hopkins in *Education World*

Ebbinghaus, H. (1885) *The hypothesis of the exponential nature of forgetting*

Ebbinghaus, H. (1885) *Memory: A contribution to experimental psychology.* New York: Dover

Friedman, T (2005). Age of Communication & Multimedia, New Definition of 'Educated' Adaptability & Lifelong Learning

Fullan, M. (2010). *All Systems Go: The Change Imperative for Whole System Reform.* Thousand Oaks: Corwin. 82 | A Rich Seam

Ramaley J. (Chair) (2002) Greater Expectations, *AACU Report.* Association of American Colleges and Universities

Tofler A. (1972) *Future Shock.* Random House

Vygotsky, L. S. (1978). *Mind in society: The development of higher psychological processes.* Cambridge, MA: Harvard University Press

Wiliam, D. (2010) The role of formative assessment in effective learning environments, in *The Nature of Learning: Using Research to Inspire Practice.* Paris: OECD Publishing

Chapter 9

A passion for excellence: leading a 'Blue Ocean' school

As educational leaders we must continually demonstrate our passion and dedication, and we must be relentless in the pursuit of achieving excellence for our students, helping them to become better than they think they can be.

Excellence can be obtained if you:

- care more than others think is wise.
- risk more than others think is safe.
- dream more than others think is practical.
- expect more than others think is possible.

Continuous evolution

The reality is that within any school we never stand still; to support our current and future success we are continuously evolving. When this happens learning improves, teaching improves, resources improve and support systems improve to the point where the quality of data and insight wholly support the notion of personalised learning for our students. Simultaneously the concept of leadership and what success is are constantly changing, constantly evolving.

Currently I find leadership discussion to be encouraging as we debate the attributes of leadership in the 21st century. Attributes for current and future leaders include: ethics, honesty, transparency, integrity, humility, respect, flexibility and collaboration. These are the foundations of our current leadership framework. Until very recently the major skills most schools focused on in their leaders were things like vision, strategic thinking, decisiveness, execution, drive, and accountability for results. While these features still remain important, it is obvious that the pendulum has swung from a focus almost purely on results to a position supporting highly ethical behaviour that still delivers. This is an extremely positive shift, one which has benefits for everyone within a school organisation, especially one which embraces distributed leadership.

The importance of setting a clear direction for a school is solidly grounded on unyielding integrity and commitment to an agreed and mutually purposeful mission. Implementation revolves around professionalism, teamwork, respect, service, and most importantly, a learning focus. However, that culture of excellence and student learning centeredness cannot be left to chance – it must be nurtured, visible and supported strongly throughout the school. This leadership style must be based on ethical values, professional integrity and drive toward a better future for all within – this will be the cornerstone for a successful school over the coming years.

A bias for action

Effective strategies for the realisation of this mission requires a bias for action, vision, articulation, moral purpose and attention to the change process in a dynamic 21st century. These are all key to the success of an effective school.

Our leadership must be accompanied by strategies which get the right people in place: people who want to make a difference and provide the energy and enthusiasm which will drive toward an identified goal – a journey which is measurable, supported by success indicators continually informing progress. Always remember that in today's fast changing, global context, within a brain-based economy, our greatest assets are our staff, their leadership potential will not emerge from a system requiring blind obedience.

The moral purpose of our leadership is to encourage everyone's evolution, as leaders we can distribute leadership and create a strong sense of moral purpose which will both mobilise and energise all, making a leap in performance, expectation and outcome.

Change as a constant feature

Change is an active and constant feature of the world in which we live. An organisation such as a school is a living thing: there is no equilibrium. The rapid nature of change in the 21st century and the non-linear nature of change have the potential to cause difficulty, particularly if we promote rigid planning and implementation expectations. Success in the 21st century is beyond planning. A flexible responsive approach to both school and human development can also provide the potential and opportunity for new paradigms, new success, new dimensions in teaching and learning and creative breakthrough to inform our activity.

We should consider moving away from a benchmarking process against the competition as the more we benchmark against our competitors, the more we risk looking like them. However we can still monitor them. We need to face up to and deal with the challenges ahead, to live with candor, without denial, to simply action toward better futures for our schools.

Our target is to create a future for our community as a 'Blue Ocean'. A Blue Ocean organisation is by definition innovative, challenging, and very successful. In our 'Blue Ocean' schools we will continually challenge and progress as learning organisations, avoiding the trap of 'this is what we do.'

There are several driving forces we are required to activate toward the creation of such a school, including technological advances, increased understanding of the learning process, growth of learning awareness and potential as well as pedagogical growth. Staff will be able to look for opportunities which further develop their skills and pedagogy beyond their current thinking and expectations and be confident in moving forward, taking risks, confident about their strengths and purpose.

Most importantly they will have a mindset founded in life-long learning, commitment to self, team and school, of being a professional educator.

As leaders our challenge is to:

- create uncontested space as a centre of excellence.
- make the competition irrelevant.
- create new paradigms in teaching and learning.

Continuously challenge, adapt and grow

As we define and develop our individual 'Blue Ocean' schools we need to be confident enough to take considered risks, to adopt a Kaizen approach of slow continuous change. Continuously challenging, adapting and growing our schools offering sustained high performance as well as increasing levels of personalisation and innovation. Concurrently we need to maintain, review and enhance rigorous and methodical approaches and systems, following key procedures relating to self evaluation, school development planning, *etc.*

We also need to be aware of, and respond flexibly and positively to, the new unforeseen opportunities that may arise. Leaders make plans, but success is often beyond planning. Ultimately our strategic plan is to get things done. We need to continue to develop a culture that has a bias for action with rapid learning, adaptation, and an appetite for challenge and change, personal and whole school improvement.

It is insufficient to only have a dream or a vision, nor is it appropriate to resist a better future because, 'this is how we do things'. We need to get things done, to execute our plans: that is the job of the leader. On our doorstep in Dubai is an outstanding example of excellent leadership encompassing, vision, execution, getting things done. HRH Sheik Rashid and HRH Sheik Mohammad have turned little known Dubai into a breathtaking display of the impossible made possible.

Dubai is the single greatest act of vision, drive and charismatic, hands on leadership, one of pure imagination. Visionary leadership combined with excellence in execution is the deepest 'Blue Ocean'.

Our mistakes will inform a better future

When we challenge, *really* challenge ourselves, it will be our mistakes which inform a new, different and better future. Our job is to encourage staff to commit to trying new ideas, bringing new learning dimensions to our students, we must continually motivate and consistently support them, to celebrate excellent failures. Then to offer to pick them up, to help them to improve and to try again, to offer the opportunity to succeed in a culture where we reward excellence and challenge mediocrity.

In summary, we need to make better mistakes. We are already transforming our learning cultures: the value recognition and support for individual differences and the growth potential for our students and staff have been areas of growing focus. Increasing personalization and assessment for learning techniques, facilitating enhanced learning styles, are now embedded in our day-to-day activity. We continue to change the way we do things, growing our capacity to seek, research, critically assess and continually incorporate best practice within and across our schools.

Across our schools we want our staff and students to have great experiences, offering added value and striving to make a difference. At best schools should be an emotional, vital, innovative, joyful, creative, entrepreneurial endeavour that elicits maximum concerted human potential in the wholehearted service of young people. Within this context every member of the school community is free to do his or her absolute best and to discover their own greatness.

We need a bias for action
To achieve this we need to acknowledge that a bias for action is essential and we need to develop a 'can do' culture where leadership matters, energy matters and tempo matters, so let's hustle! We can ride the value-added curve to the sky but to do so we need to distribute leadership, energise, listen, challenge, and grow excellence in an environment where everyone is a leader, where schools are great places to be and work! As we continually strive for excellence and continually redefine success we create an 'excellence always' culture to the benefit of every student and member of staff. Deep 'Blue Ocean!'

References and further reading
Claxton, C. (2002) *Building Learning Power: Helping Young People Become Better Learners*. Bristol: TLO

Dryden, G. and Vos, J. (2005) *The New Learning Revolution*. 3rd Edition

Kim, W. C. & Mauborgne, R. (2005) *Blue Ocean Strategy*. Boston, MA: Harvard Business School Pub

Chapter 10

The power and potential of play

by Ruth Burke

Play is a hugely influential aspect of learning in children. When left to their own devices, children can effectively imagine, create and solve problems, reproduce real and fictitious places and scenarios. Children readily communicate and create, negotiate and collaborate and engage with their surroundings and with each other. The playfulness that children exhibit encompasses social, cognitive, cultural and affective elements of development.

Opportunities for children to play at their own level of complexity, with varying degrees of challenge, develop naturally while children interact and learn to negotiate with others. Pretend, role, dramatic and socio-dramatic play provides opportunities for children to create and influence outcomes of versions of their own social and emotional experiences and to vary levels of challenge while providing teachers with in-depth information about their understanding and learning. We must never lose sight of, nor underestimate, the power and the potential of play in children of any age.

Some things about children become so familiar to us that we lose sight of how remarkable they are – and lose sight too, of how little we understand the processes that underlie developmental achievements. (Hobson, 2002: 5)

A driving force in learning

In my work as a teacher, lead learner and headteacher, the one constant driving force is to maximise learning opportunities and learning potential. In my role of parent, the driving force is not dissimilar – I wish for the exuberant passion and curiosity that my young adult offspring exhibit for their chosen courses of study to last forever. For my toddler, his natural curiosity and desire to explore and investigate every facet of life – authentic learning at its best – continues to remind me that in those in between years of 18 months to 18 years, children must be empowered to be excited, curious and active in their quest to learn.

The levels of curiosity, creativity and deep engagement exhibited by a group of youngsters, so totally absorbed in play in a home corner setting in Foundation Two for example, where no matter what else is happening in that room, they remain focused and fully engaged, needs to be the norm for engagement levels in all classrooms, school-wide. In developing opportunities for pupils to play throughout the primary school and beyond, we will be adding to opportunities for real life, deep learning.

Solving real life problems though play

As children develop though the primary phase, teachers must seek to avoid losing the natural playfulness that exists in children. Themes and topics can and must be brought to life, abstract concepts and ideas explored and deepened, written composition prepared through acting out scenarios and real life problems solved, through play opportunities. Three characteristics for good learning in history, according to Fines and Nichol (1997) are that 'it must excite and entice children and be theirs, it must be true and honour the past, it must leave you understanding yourself and the present a lot better'.

In a Year 4 shared area, a group of children, observed recently, are deep in discussion. Over the previous couple of weeks they had set up a Viking museum, comprising of:

- an entrance where the curator shares an overview of Viking times.
- an interactive theatre where actors, after performing selected sketches showcasing aspects of the life and times of the Vikings, (including

information on costume, food, shelter, raids and conquests), interact with the audience.

- an exhibition of Viking artefacts some with written explanations and others brought to life through iMovies and Aurasma with iPads available for the children to use.

- a computer section where the visitors to the museum are invited to give feedback on their Viking experience by completing questionnaires (designed by the children) on Google forms and Survey Monkey.

Learning through play is not restricted to the primary phase of education. One of the best history lessons I have seen, involved a secondary school teacher donning his cloak and crown, sitting on his throne and explaining the facts of medieval life to the peasants in his domain. The results were staggering in terms of engagement and deep learning with students who, later in the project, were able and willing to 'hot seat', collaborate, engage in role play and keen to further research the subject.

Role play and active engagement
As well as great learning in history, this area has been developed with the addition of new scenarios, developing the scope of the children's play.

A new exhibition opening night, for example, gave our budding event managers and journalists great scope for creativity, whilst treasure stolen from the museum saw investigation teams and detectives hard at work. The children were empowered to make suggestions, source props, conduct research, contribute and manage displays, suggest new scenarios and set the ground rules for the area, demonstrating great levels of enthusiasm and interest whilst assuming leadership roles as necessary. Collaboration, negotiation, communication and participation were observed and before long the pupils were deeply engaged in sharing and developing their learning of the Vikings. High quality, meaningful learning was facilitated through play-based opportunities. Pupil engagement levels were high within a multidisciplinary approach ensuring pupils had options and scope to develop not only their interest in history, but to develop thinking skills and learning-to-learn skills.

Similarly, the quality of the written work produced by our Year 6 pupils learning about World War Two, following a whole year group re-enactment of an evacuation where children was superb. They were asked to return to school one evening with an overnight bag, arriving to the sound of sirens, transported to an neighbouring school where they were lined up, inspected, allocated new homes and families and later returned to their school hall to spend the night. Their diary-entry writing and letters home were hugely enhanced by the experience; the sharing of artefacts, photos, war songs and soup and bread for their tea brought the subject matter to life and engaged the pupils in a play-based scenario.

The role play following the World War Two evening, where children packed suitcases as evacuees, created ration books, researched and created gas masks and such like all for use in the role play area was perceptive and inspired. The children themselves when questioned on the experience described their evacuation experience as "something they would remember always", "a great way to experience how evacuees might feel" and "it makes you get an idea of how refugees we see on TV must feel when they are forced to leave their homes".

Get real!
Domestic-based role play is most often seen as the domain of the Early Years but I would urge teachers working with older children to allow for this type of play too. From working out relationship and communication issues to trying out alternative roles, characters and approaches, there is much to be gained by older primary children having access to versions of home-centred play opportunities.

Similarly in the Early Years, providing scope for a range of scenarios is beneficial. The science laboratory in our Foundation Two classroom where children were encouraged to dress, behave, think and work as real scientists, saw our pupils interact with bicarbonate of soda and a range of different strength acids, investigate acid base chemistry using red cabbage juice and discover the effects of detergent on surface tension using milk and food colouring. The children found out, through investigative play, what did and didn't cause a reaction; they asked searching questions and made informed deductions based on their observations.

The role of the adult in play
Over many years in the field of primary education, I have observed role play from a range of perspectives. Indeed, my earliest memory of my own primary schooling aged four, is myself playing in a role play shop – immersion in retail from an early age! In the successful role play I observe now, adults play a pivotal but highly flexible role.

The most challenging element for the adult is always whether/when to intervene, if at all. For sure, modelling play can be useful sometimes when introducing a new subject, but should never be at the expense of limiting children's own creativity or spontaneity. Sometimes adults are required to intervene to manage disputes but again should do so sparingly. What can appear to be 'misbehaviour, chaos and conflict can act as a platform for play to become increasingly challenging and complex' (Broadhead, 2009).

Crucially, play requires resourcing; staff must be highly resourceful in acquiring or creating the necessary 'stuff' for any role play area. Staff need to be highly communicative too, openly demonstrating value for pupil voice – children love to be involved in the planning, resourcing and setting up of a new area in their classroom. Being open to suggestions and willing to make changes to the planning is key. In order to enhance learning and engage all learners, taking on the suggestions of the end users will pay dividends – so ensure that pupils have their say!

Observation of pupils engaged in role play, whatever their age, will enable adults to reflect, collaborate and plan next steps in learning. This assessment and evaluation should have a knowledge function, enabling practitioners to develop informed insights into a child's patterns and styles of learning and an auditing function providing summative information about a child's achievements and competencies (Wood and Attfield, 2005: 185).

Play can enhance children's understanding of their immediate world, and it can support pupils' understanding of abstract concepts and unfamiliar environments. Play engages and empowers learners and enables great scope in designing multi-disciplinary projects which can lead to deeper learning. Play can provide meaningful insights in to pupils' perceptions and progress. In addition, children love to play; they are naturally motivated and curious in their play. We must never lose sight of how powerful and potent play in the primary school can be.

References and further reading

Beardsley, G. (1998) *Exploring Play in the Primary Classroom.* London: D. Fulton Publishers

Broadhead, P. and Burt, A. (2012) *Understanding Young Children's Learning through Play.* London: Routledge

Fines J. and Nichol, J. (1997) *Teaching Primary History.* Oxford: Heinemann

Hobson, P. (2002) *The Cradle of Thought: Exploring the Origins of Thinking.* Basingstoke: MacMillan

Rogers, S. and Evans, J. (2008) *Inside Role-Play in Early Childhood Education.* London: Routledge

Wood, E. and Attfield, J. (2005) *Play, Learning and the Early Childhood Curriculum.* London: PCP

Chapter 11

Seeking the expert: teachers who recognise the moment

As we continue to develop our schools we occasionally need to 'shift the lens' to consider and support our educators as they become deeply engaged in professional learning with the aim of developing pedagogic experts who will inform enhance pupil learning, progress and achievement. 'Teacher expertise is the most important factor in improving students' learning.' (Darling *et al*, 1999). In acknowledging that as an evolving practice teaching undergoes constant change, our obligation to our profession and to every student is to encourage all staff to attend to their expertise, to become continual learners in their own right.

This is a vehicle for whole school improvement to improve teacher potential and enhance students' opportunities and achievement. According to Walsh (2007) the odds that a child will have a great teacher five years in a row are one in 17,000. Five great teachers in a row would be something special for any school, for any student.

Professional learning
There are constraints, the legitimacy of habit and, yes, we are busy. However, we can create space for professional learning, to encourage our educators to continually progress and up-skill themselves over the course of their careers. Malcolm Gladwell (2008) claims it takes 10,000 hours of sustained and deliberate practice to become an expert in a

particular 'skill' – that's about a decade for a teacher. Deliberate practice is a considered choice requiring an individual educator to invest specific and sustained effort at what one is not (yet) good at and pushing self-limitations (Ericsson *et al*, 2007).

As school leaders we cannot leave this to chance; a clear focus to professional learning is essential if we are to develop these focused educators and talented professionals who have the potential to inspire and advantage every student in our charge. That is our moral imperative if we are to grow the potential of, and empower our young people.

For any successful school the intention is to enhance your positive learning culture with strong and purposeful professional learning, accepting always that professional learning is a gradual uneven process which can have a flow of its own. Professional teachers do not develop automatically as a consequence of being. The drive to improve and to have a positive influence on student learning requires passion, patience, and attention to detail.

On this journey toward becoming an expert teacher, developing expert traits our educators must have the courage to continually challenge themselves, to take risks, to refuse to be complacent. Educator thinking, talent and teaching skills require development and refinement over time as we continually apply our professional judgement in order to respond to the learning needs and concerns of our students on a day-to-day basis.

Expert teachers matter

Recognising our expert teachers matter requires understanding and defining what we mean by the term 'expert teacher'. A key task is the determination of assessment criteria so that the professional competence of teachers can be evaluated. Once these exceptional teachers or exceptional traits are identified, we need to highlight and share their expertise with colleagues. Such teachers have the potential to inspire, to support and develop other educators, with the aim of supporting the growth of every student.

Our first questions need to consider what knowledge, skills and personal attributes our teachers require today and will need for tomorrow. Teaching has always been and will always be complex work, but expert teachers work at levels well beyond the technical. However, technical competence is the sure base from which expertise grows. Expert teachers are driven for excellence, they continually think, discuss and challenge in order that their work better aligns learning and teaching. Expert teachers make the complex act of teaching look easy.

It's not easy, of course. Nothing could be further from the truth! Danielson (1996) estimated that a teacher makes more than 3,000 non-trivial decisions every day. The subtlety, timeliness and preparedness of these interventions, improvised responses, instantly phrased questions all outline the true complexity of a teacher's work. So what are we looking for? Brett *et al* (2009: 15) indicated that expert attributes encompassed elements such as:

- knowledge (knowing what)
- attitudes and behaviours (being aware of how we act, in context and why)
- dispositions (being open to change, feeling motivation)
- procedural skills (knowing how to do)
- cognitive skills (treating information, critical thinking and critical analysis)
- experiential skills (to know how to react and adapt on the basis of previous knowledge, social skills)

Expert teachers are problem-solvers

Among many indicators, Hattie (2003) notes that:

> Expert teachers have deeper representations about teaching and learning. Expert teachers adopt a problem-solving stance to their work. Expert teachers are adept at monitoring student problems and assessing their level of understanding and progress, and they provide much more relevant, useful feedback. Expert teachers are passionate about teaching and learning.

There are professional skills sets, there is professional knowledge but alongside this we are discussing the deep complexity and consequences of human relationships against the background of a fast changing 21st century. All too often in researching this area profound thinkers come up with lists of attributes; however, the personal attributes of expert teachers, their beyond-professional attributes and the variety of contexts in which they work make such lists limiting; attitudes may be more important. As individuals they want to grow, energising themselves with new research, new technology and educational tools which inform better teaching and better learning.

Effective 21st century teachers use a variety of media in their lessons supporting today's students who were born in the digital age, they have embraced technological advancement as we all should. In doing so this variety of media allows them to present information in a clear manner, combine words with pictures, use various teaching aids and maximise teaching time.

Aligning leaning intentions

Expert teachers ensure that their teaching intentions align with the learning intentions they have for their pupils and have a great depth of content knowledge that is organised in ways that reflect detailed understanding of their subject matter. In monitoring learning they are sensitised to noticing and make informed, positive interventions, applying a dynamic relationship between their assessment of students' learning and their planning of the next learning step.

These highly effective educators are proactive rather than reactive: they plan ahead, carefully considering the learning pathway, creatively formulating or seeking out solutions to solve potential problems. Expert teachers have high expectations for their students and insist on promoting learning for all students. They are intellectual leaders, reflective and driven to improve outcomes, they also tend to be more effective (McBer, 2000).

The quantity and variety of knowledge expert teachers have about individual students can be staggering, varying from family situation, academic effort, motivation, learning styles, physical development and cognitive processing. It is the links they make between these different types of knowledge which ensures a teacher's effectiveness. This allows expert teachers to actively facilitate learning as they integrate standards, skills, concepts, and knowledge regularly in learning-focused projects that engage, motivate and respond to student needs, passions and interests. It is also worth noting that our expert teachers are also our best report writers as they know their learners so well.

Optimising student learning

Above all else expert teachers know what they are doing and why (Loughran, 2010); they have the ability to optimise students' learning. Expert teachers seek challenges, learn from mistakes, and keep faith in themselves in the face of failure, which is viewed as an opportunity to learn.

They are inspirational, ensuring that their teaching intentions are focused on the learning expectations they have for all students, inspiring their natural curiosity. Their technical skills are highly tuned to create effective learning. Expert teachers choose activities for a learning purpose and are transparent with students about this purpose. They carefully think and plan for learning, considering how to structure their teaching in ways that will have a positive influence on students' learning, personal and academic progress.

Experience and professional knowledge allows expert teachers to recognise opportunities and act. They are highly aware, monitoring and adjusting the pace of learning, providing corrective feedback and ensure that the invitation to learning is open to everyone. Crucially they recognise and meet students at their point of confusion and can draw upon a range of intervention strategies. They require students to think deeply, are demanding of students and develop strong conceptual understanding and deep intellectual engagement. They demonstrate emotional awareness, continually recognising and praising students' strategies, focus, effort, persistence, and improvement: they are consistently outstanding over time.

Expert teachers create stimulating learning environments, they are perceptive and understand the dynamics of the classroom, and they take the time to build an environment conducive to optimal education.

It is not just the physical environment that will offer recognition to students and their work, stimulation of curiosity and creativity, reflection upon past work and an insight into future learning: all of which are valuable and potent. It is also about creating a learning ethos: an environment where constantly checking for understanding is embedded, where the teacher is a role model knowledgeable and confident, well informed about student capability and is able to turn control over to the learners.

In managing this environment these teachers demonstrate their awareness of the importance of student conceptual understanding and of student intellectual engagement. This environment is managed with skill, highly attuned to the needs of the group and the individual learners within it.

Teachers of the highest calibre know how to ensure that students speak up honestly, and safely saying what they think. They consider questions carefully; maintain an open, questioning approach, with extended questioning techniques encouraging students to explain their thinking. It's not about being right or wrong – the mindset is about wanting to understand the students' thinking and their depth of understanding.

This environment not only offers great questions, it allows for and encourages the students to ask good questions and challenge, in an atmosphere of mutual respect, responding to one another's point of view.

> Students who are taught by expert teachers exhibit an understanding of the concepts targeted in instruction that is more integrated, more coherent, and at a higher level of abstraction than the understanding achieved by other students (Hattie, 2003).

Expert teachers are continuous, life-long learners; they remain alert intellectually and open to responsible change grounded in theory, research, and practice. They explore the potential of new technologies, cooperative learning, diversity, assessment and evaluation, rubrics, closing the achievement gap, creativity and curriculum reform. All this because they love to teach, they continuously strive to improve, Dylan Wiliam (2013); concurs: 'Every teacher needs to improve, not because they are not good enough, but because they can be even better'.

Many personal attributes also inform expertness as well as the varying context in which every teacher works as well as a holistic approach to the job. To be an expert teacher is to forever be a work in progress. Happy in their work, these teachers are drivers, self-effacing and dedicated to the betterment of others, continually teaching great lessons, striving for excellence, Specifically, it's an issue of building capacity; teacher knowledge and expertise (Callahan, Griffo, & Pearson, 2009).

These teachers offer high levels of care. Their understanding and celebration of learning and achievement is exceptional, taking the time to get to know their students as learners and people, relating effectively to all. As passionate educators they are aware that individuals learn differently, they are able to select and utilize strategies to differentiate and personalise opportunities to learn and succeed, adapting to meet their students capability and need.

They are willing to be creative and adaptive, daring to think outside the box for the benefit of their students. Providing the most expert instruction and support possible demands is 'a level of collegiality and collaboration that many schools have not realized' (Costello *et al,* 2010). Identification and recognition of such attributes in our teachers will be highly motivational for those on this pathway, additionally we will have the opportunity to enable them to collaborate and work across classrooms, to connect with peers to enhance the capabilities of all.

Are we up for the challenge? I hope so.

References and further reading

Brett, P., Mompoint-Gaillard, P., & Salema, M. H. (2009). *How all teachers can support citizenship and human rights education: a framework for the development of competences.* Strasbourg: Council of Europe Publishing

Callahan, M., Griffo, V. & Pearson, P.D. (2009). *Teacher knowledge & teaching reading.* College Reading Association Yearbook

Costello, K. A., Lipson, M. Y., Marinak, B., and Zolman, M. F. (2010). *New roles for educational leaders: Starting and sustaining a systemic approach to RTI*

Danielson, C. (1996) *Enhancing professional practice: A framework for teaching.* Alexandria, VA: Association for Supervision and Curriculum Development

Ericsson, A., Prietula, Michael J., Cokely, Edward T. (2007) The Making of an Expert. *Harvard Business Review*

Gladwell, M. (2008) *Outliers: The Story of Success.* Barnes & Noble

Hattie, J. (2003) *Teachers Make a Difference.* Australian Council for Educational Research, Melbourne

Loughran, J. (2010) *Expert teachers.* NEITA Teaching Awards – Keynote Speech

McBer, H. (2000) *Research into teacher effectiveness: a model of teacher effectiveness.* Research report 216. DfEE

Turner-Bisset, R. (1999) The knowledge bases of the expert Teacher. *British Educational Research Journal,* 25 (1) p. 39-55

Walsh, K (2007) *If Wishes Were Horses: The Reality Behind Teacher Quality Ratings,* National Council on Teacher Quality, Washington DC

Wiliam, D (2013) *Teacher quality: Why it matters and how to get more of it.* Institute of Education, University of London

Chapter 12

Great teachers and great questions

Great teachers dare to excel and have the audacity to be brilliant; they are the drivers, the energisers, and the lifeblood of any school. Their measured work and the decisions they make on a day-to-day basis have a profound impact upon the lives of young people and it must never be forgotten that the success of any school comes from teachers who deliberately activate learning. The best have a work ethic that doesn't waver, they have steadiness of purpose, they are dedicated and driven; their dedication and professionalism is what makes the difference.

A culture of integrity

The best teachres inspire optimism, developing a culture of integrity, responding seriously to students and constantly building their confidence. An effective teacher makes their craft appear effortless and seamless; they are often found in schools where there is positive and thoughtful leadership which provides a purposeful and stable environment. These leaders create an aspirant, 'can do' learning-focused environment, one which values pupil voice and is supportive in culturing self-belief and confidence.

'There is no denying the pivotal role of the Headteacher in creating the ethos of the school and in exercising strong pedagogical leadership' (*Twenty Successful Primary Schools in Challenging Circumstances*, Ofsted, 2009).

It is important for any school to have an ethos in which every pupil is valued, motivated and confident and where educators feel supported and able to innovate and take risks. These activators of learning spend most of their lives in front of students, they enjoy the company of others and more often lean toward the fellowship of others; they are intellectually alive, responsive and positive, dedicated to their craft.

Great teaching is easy to recognise, but hard to define. The truth is there is no one-size-fits-all for great teaching especially when you factor in the impact of individual circumstances and context.

Teaching is a complicated task, it demands broad knowledge of subject matter, curriculum, and standards; enthusiasm, a caring attitude, and a love of learning. Great teachers have high expectations, encourage curiosity and engender high levels of engagement which impact positively upon the quality of learning of pupils; learning experiences which make a difference to the lives of young people.

Teachers embrace every day with a mix of expectation, preparation, and flexibility, the best are willing to take risks and do things differently in order to meet the diverse needs of their students, offering a mix of learning approaches accommodating different learning styles and intelligences. This positive mindset motivates them to advocate for great teaching and learning every lesson in every day, these driven day-to-day interfaces offer opportunity for every student to engage and progress.

An intentional growth process

Becoming a great teacher isn't something that happens overnight, there is no course or single transformational experience which can create an educator. Teacher development is an intentional growth process which begins with a very deliberate decision to serve others. Drawing on the ever-deepening connection to the students we serve, we continually study, practice, reflect and grow as we nurture an extraordinary commitment to continually do the best we can for others.

First things first: students always come first. A key trait in every effective educator is to continually support students to make good choices, offering seamless and meaningful support; we are available to them, striving to understand their joy, their challenges and their concerns. This is the essence of a student-centered approach that makes their needs, within and beyond the curriculum, a priority. Educators commit career long to improve their pedagogy for the good of young people. Effective teachers spend a lot of time learning with their peers continually informing their professional growth, discovering new ways to enrich learning experiences, in the background of their lives a constant echo for change.

Great teachers engage with professional learning communities within their schools, in addition the best will be outward-looking as linking well with colleagues beyond their immediate environment. These educators create a climate of community; they are great connectors and are continually collaborating with colleagues to enhance and redesign the delivery of their professional learning.

This act of sharing and engaging is fuelled by reading, researching, engaging with colleagues, investing time and knowledge with colleagues who have an affiliation with their passion and vision. These teachers demonstrate a collective commitment to better learning in collaborative settings, continually reflecting, sharing, listening and learning allows great teachers to awaken their individual potential.

Developing as thinking leaders, they have the courage to take meaningful risks which lead to higher impact in terms of teaching and learning. They are aware of who and what they are as professional educators, leaders of learning who continually inform sustainable change for the benefit and growth of our students.

Inspiring students to take risks

Effective teaching will challenge and enthuse pupils, and assessment will indicate that students are actively engaged in their learning and are making progress. Great teachers offer opportunities which inspire students to take risks, make connections in their learning encouraging students to develop through collaboration or independent learning. Effective teachers have the ability, energy and the acumen to hold students' attention through subject mastery, skillful lesson structure which is built upon a detailed awareness of the material to be taught, they demonstrate caring, and an honesty that reveals their individual personality.

It is difficult to define a list of the characteristic of an effective teacher as without question it is a complex act. As previously mentioned, Danielson (1996) estimates that a teacher makes more than 3,000 non-trivial decisions every day. Very few jobs demand such a capacity for instant decision making and subtlety of application which is an outcome of so many unique interactions. How to frame a responsive question? To be agile, thinking on your feet: indeed teachers are highly skilled, knowledgeable and gifted learners themselves, intelligent concerned interested and interesting.

Questioning is the major vehicle for learning

Questioning is the major vehicle for learning and knowledge transfer in our classrooms. It is an essential part of an engaging learning environment, encouraging student progress by eliciting thinking which informs student engagement and assessment opportunities which inform great teaching.

The art of asking questions is an essential element of good teaching and one of the basic skills all teachers are required to master as they ask up to two questions every minute, and 70,000 a year with a potential for two to three million in the course of a career. If you are going to ask so many questions you need to be purposeful and learn to ask the right questions, the right way at the right time. The best educators also find opportunities for students to raise their questions. We also need to access a wide variety of questioning styles, especially when you consider that questioning accounts for one third of all teaching time.

We also need to give more time when questioning, the average time we wait for a response is only one second, we need to extend our wait time.

Questions serve many purposes and are an essential component of any lesson. Teachers use questions to engage students and sustain an 'active' style to the learning, they also use questions as an assessment tool; questions may also be used to inspire learning. The how and why we use questions in the classroom informs the flow of the lesson, engages students in their learning and provides opportunities for them to share their opinions, seeking the views of others. As well as being a tool for assessment, great questions encourage thinking and creativity; they foster hypothesis and idea forming in a context of shared learning.

Being thoughtful and intentional

Effective questioning involves the teacher's ability to construct and dispense well-considered questions as well as their ability to provide answers. They are thoughtful and intentional, able to anticipate potential responses and are deliberate as they use questions to drive and inform discovery and learning. The best will model and offer thinking time, allowing participants to be more considered in their responses. This will encourage increased participation from students who will in return phrase responses which are longer, more creative and have a greater level of analysis.

When engaged in this way students offer more questions as well as demonstrating greater reflection. Offering a more patient approach allows learners to contribute to the groups understanding, allowing active listening, higher levels of concentration and every student feeling valued.

The two most common forms of questions are closed and open. Closed or convergent questions are a way to find a specific answer usually in one or two words, useful for simple recall or to determine student understanding. If you want students to think this style of question is not effective, then we turn to open-ended or divergent questions to encourage authentic reflection and discussion. Open-ended questions are powerful as they encourage natural learning through exploration, reflection and discovery. They build upon previous learning inviting students to access their own curiosity with teachers encouraging confidence and competence leading to higher levels of active learning and engagement.

Open-ended questions open the door for teachers to demonstrate their own curiosity and their genuine interest in their students' answers. This extension of trust empowers students to engage at a deeper level. reasoning and reflecting and, crucially, thinking for themselves as they collaborate, interact and learn from one another.

Hinge questions instigate thinking
Hinge questions or hinge point questions offer the opportunity for a classroom discussion to move forward in at least two different directions. This is a short question focused upon a key concept which allows the teacher to see who gets it, measuring the students' collective response which in turn influences the direction of discussion.

Like all good questions they instigate thinking and open the door to more questions as students seek to clarify understanding allowing for a 'think, pair, share' approach amongst others. For a direction to be determined a hinge point question must be based on a concept in a lesson that is important and it must build upon what the students already know. It also allows the teacher to offer tailored questions, clearly differentiated to the knowledge, needs and interests of students.

These are powerful questions which can lead to high impact learning as well as clarifying understanding for students and informing teachers awareness of student learning as all are required to respond. Usually a hinge question is offered around the mid- point in a lesson, a focused question that can raise several responses, all of which can be agreed, defended or discussed further. They are formative, enabling educators and students to engage in the key area of evidence gathering and interpretation, a key process at the heart of learning.

An example of this could be: "When did the Second World War start? 1919, 1934 or 1939?" Students' responses to this will vary according to their knowledge and insight. In listening to the response of others they will meet differing perspectives, this will help them to reflect on their own understanding, creating an opportunity for further discussion and research which will ideally lead to a deeper understanding and uniquely individual responses.

These questions are initially challenging for students as they are uniquely difficult for teachers to phrase, and as a teacher you will need to be on your toes, you need to respond quickly. However the learning potential they offer is invaluable. Although hinge questions take time to generate, a good question will still be useful in the 20 years' time, because learners will still face the same difficulties they do now' (Wiliam, 2011: 100). They offer opportunities for assessment opportunities founded in both knowledge and cognition, giving you insight into which students have got a critical concept and which haven't. Students are both challenged and engaged by hinge questions, sharing and moving forward together, deepening and extending knowledge and understanding on the basis of what they already know.

Essentially a hinge question is a vehicle which quickly gives the teacher and learner a point at which they can determine what they know and embark upon the next stage in learning; crucially they allow the context for alternative conceptions, sharing and collaboration as they seek to develop and deepen understanding.

Great questions open doors to learning

Great questions open the door for teachers to demonstrate their own curiosity and their genuine interest in students' answers. Thought-provoking questions can get learners talking, discussing, reflecting, and writing their thoughts – this is when students actively engage and gain ownership of their learning.

A cautionary note: be careful, even the best questions can lead to answers which surprise and challenge even the best. When this happens be humble, remember it's about them not you, take the opportunity to engage with your students in the cognitive domain. Go for it alongside them and continue to phrase and apply powerful questions – you never know what you might learn.

References and further reading

Canter, L., & Canter, M. (2002) *Assertive discipline: Positive behavior management for today's classroom* (3rd ed.). Los Angeles: Lee Canter & Associates

Danielson, C. (1996). *Enhancing professional practice: A framework for teaching.* Alexandria, VA: Association for Supervision and Curriculum Development

Erickson, H. L. (2007) *Concept-based curriculum and instruction for the thinking classroom.* Thousand Oaks, CA. Corwin Press

Goldberg, M. (1990). Portrait of Madeline Hunter. *Educational Leadership,* 47(5), p. 41–43

Kohn, A. (1996). *Beyond discipline: From compliance to community.* Alexandria, VA: Association for Supervision and Curriculum Development

Ofsted, Dr Peter Matthews, (2009) *Twenty Successful Primary Schools in Challenging Circumstances.* www.ofsted.gov.uk/publications

Wiliam, Dylan (2011): *Embedded Formative Assessment.* Perfect Paperback

Chapter 13

Transformational Leadership: Philosophy, Pedagogy and Courage

by Shabnam Cadwallender

The following is less about extolling the virtues of any one style of leadership or proclaiming creativity in the design of a curriculum, but more about having courage of conviction and unleashing bravery in the people around you.

JUST DO IT. That's what Nike implore you to do. Forget how hard it is going to be, how long and steep the road ahead is, forget what else is going on around you. Believe in yourself: just do it.

In my five years as head teacher and the eleven years preceding that as a class teacher, my conscience would always tell me to 'just do it'. To believe that what I knew was right and trust the knowledge I'd accumulated in order to make a difference to the pupils I had in my care; and not only the pupils but their families and my colleagues. As a British-Bangladeshi, brought up in the North-East of England, non-conformity was a byword for the way I lived my life, and as an educator I was a quiet maverick. My desire to 'boldly go' often forced me to surreptitiously avoid what I knew was ineffective methodology and slip in my own pedagogy behind a closed classroom door.

As a transformational leader, the ultimate goal is to motivate people and to get them to think for themselves (Schultz & Schultz, 2008); to muster that inner sense of ambition, unbuckle the straightjacket that so many teachers feel they are constrained by and ... just do it.

Seeking new horizons

This is no conjecture. I was the teacher who felt like a caged bird, unable to spread my wings freely; those wings that had not been clipped by my own education or my training to become a teacher. The desire to lead a school was partly borne out of my own frustrations with existing leadership; their lack of courage and either their misunderstanding of how children learn or, worse, a blatant disregard for it. It seemed that some school leaders were content with their completed visions of the future, fuelled by one or more of the initiatives handed to them by spin doctors based on an ever increasing chasm between the real world and learning.

There was no real sense of perpetual improvement, even though lifelong learning was a buzz phrase. It was my wanderlust that kept me asking questions and seeking new horizons in all aspects of my life. This restlessness is what keeps successful leaders and schools flourishing and is the "key to reinvigorating any business. Otherwise, stagnation beckons." (Blatchford, 2014).

Perfection is just around the corner

When I became a head teacher, stagnation was something I was adamant about avoiding. But stagnation can be so subtle and creep up on an organisation. Even in schools where leadership is considered thorough, focussed on outcomes with rigorous monitoring and clear target setting, learning and, more importantly, the desire to learn, can languish. Blatchford asserts that the "knowledge that perfection is just around the corner" is what is needed to keep schools striving to improve. However I suspect that for some leaders, this end result, or the fear of it, is what actually causes inertia within their organisations.

In my first week of headship I was told by staff that they had no wish to become outstanding; my predecessor had sought to enlighten them in the ways of Ofsted and they weren't interested. Like many teachers, they felt that perfection was not attainable on a daily basis, they rejected any criticism of their practice and found solace in 'playing the game' whilst doing their own thing in the classroom. The result? Stagnation; in the progress made by pupils, the methodology employed by staff to deliver the curriculum and in active participation amongst pupils. There is a quote, by some American football coach I think, which highlights the fact that attaining perfection is not the actual goal but that in its pursuance, excellence is achieved.

Perceptions of perfection

My challenge was to change their perceptions of what perfection was; enjoy the chase and reinvigorate their passion for learning through my leadership, my convictions and my relationships with them (Harris, 2012). Relationships can be tricky at best, but the relationship a Head has with their staff is crucial, paving the way for all relationships within a school community (Barth, 1990). If it's an open and honest relationship acknowledging that mistakes are part of the journey and that no one can know everything or get it right first time, then both parties will be willing to go the extra mile in pursuit of improving the learning climate and outcomes for all.

Focus on learning … everyone's learning

But creating such an honest and open relationship can be fraught with pitfalls. It would be easy for a young, new Head to appear patronising. So rather than focussing on the staff themselves, what was needed was a focus on learning...everyone's learning, not just that of the pupils (Knapp et al, 2010). Making every snippet of conversation, every formal meeting and every documented communication about learning and how it could be improved was the way in which staff began to feel less personally scrutinised and more accountable for whole school improvement. This shift made it possible for me to dare them to dare themselves, made it possible for them to be courageous practitioners.

Unleashing bravery in those around you can only be productive, however, if there is a common vision, otherwise what you could end up with is a team of mavericks all chasing their own passionate goals. To this end, having a shared educational philosophy with agreed outcomes is paramount. Clarity of vision is cited by many as being a critical factor of excellent leadership, but, as I alluded to earlier, visions have the tendency to be static and can be incredibly subjective. Much better then to have clarity of philosophy and pedagogy which allows teachers to have the autonomy they seek, indeed which they deserve, without subverting the agreed outcomes.

In order to ensure its philosophy is united, that it permeates all levels and is seen through every interaction, a school needs to know what is at the centre of that philosophy. Securing educational philosophy is not unlike the way a company such as Nike develops and maintains its branding. But we are no multi-national corporation, just a very small rural school, and in being such we target a small customer base, ensuring that our 'brand' is relevant, compelling and sustainable (Gerver, 2010)

In an increasingly high-stakes game of accountability and with an ever tightening grip on curricula, having a personal educational philosophy that can be enacted is not child's play. However, when that philosophy is shared and articulated amongst all of those within an establishment and championed by courageous leadership, it becomes intrinsic (Waters, 2013).

Getting to that point is not easy, particularly when faced with teachers who have been constrained and placed in a box, doubtful of their own professionalism and de-skilled. Staff need to rediscover what it means to teach, what learning looks like, and know that they are trusted by going beyond the curriculum and the barriers of data-driven schooling. That is not to say that accountability and achievement should be precluded, nor is it that curricula are irrelevant: the opposite is, in fact, true.

Learning is multi-dimensional
In enacting educational philosophy, staff need to embrace accountability and see it as a way of informing the progress of all: a brave step for many, viewing monitoring and tracking as a professional dialogue, where their insight as well as performance is valued. Additionally, in order to contradict the view that standards in schools can be elevated by implementing system after system, which propagates the notion that our pupils are statistics, it is important to make a shift towards the view that monitoring is a way of gathering comprehensive information, rather than data. This highlights the multi-dimensional aspects of learning that cannot be described by a numeric level alone.

This shift also allows teachers to use their knowledge and understanding of how children learn in order to affect a greater rate of progress. Staff become true leaders of learning, turning less to generic one-size-fits-all strategies and focussing instead on personalised agenda for improvement (Hattie, 2012). They become braver at seeking and using innovative practice around them, and adapting it to fit the pupils in their care; at using research to fuel new ideas within school and evaluate each other to ensure astute progress for their pupils (Blatchford, 2014)

To boldly go...

In my five years as a head teacher, I have striven to continue my desire to boldly go, to provide the best learning conditions for the pupils, families and colleagues in my care. But now I am no longer alone on that journey. Actually, I don't think I ever was. It is clear to me now that leadership is about maximising the efforts of those around you, unleashing their bravery.

As the road before the runner in the Nike shoes continues to rise, it challenges them to keep on running, to push their own levels of fitness and capability. We as educators will continue to embrace the paradox that we exist in; knowing we have secure values and aims, and yet also to seek to keep up with the pace of change. We should search for new challenges and challenge new problems, courageous in our desire to make the right difference for the pupils in our trust.

References and further reading

Barth, R. S. (1990). *Improving Schools from Within: Teachers, Parents, and Principles Can Make a Difference.* San Francisco, CA: Jossey-Bass

Blatchford, R. (2014). *The Restless School.* Woodbridge: John Catt Educational Ltd

Gerver, R. (2010). *Creating Tomorrow's School Today.* Continuum International Publishing Group

Harris, D. (2012). *Brave Heads: How to Lead a School Without Selling Your Soul*

Hattie, J. (2012). *Visible Learning for Teachers, Maximizing impact on learning.* London: Routledge

Knapp, M., Copland, M., Honig, M., Plecki, M., Portin, B. (2010). *Learning-focused Leadership and Leadership Support: Meaning and Practice in Urban Systems.* University of Washington: The Wallace Foundation

Schultz, D. & Schultz, S. (2008). *Theories of Personality.* Wadsworth Publishing Co.

Waters, M. (2013). *Thinking Allowed on Schools.* Independent Thinking Press

Chapter 14

The learning disconnect

Rapid globalisation is offering challenges to all of us. We live in a world of technological change, diverse and interconnected populations and the availability of vast amounts of information and knowledge. Today there are about 17 billion devices connected to the internet. Today things are moving quickly, so much so that we now effectively have a 'learning disconnect'. This is when a student says: "Every time I go to school I have to power down." For us as educators this just doesn't add up; on a daily basis we acknowledge, encourage and celebrate the fact that our students learn in different ways and more often we are personalising their learning.

Mobile-learning connects our students to their peers; it continually challenges them with real-world information and engages them in real time, real-world conversations.

A decade of transformational change

Classrooms have gone through transformational change in the past decade. The entire body of human knowledge can be accessed in any room. Today the world has become the curriculum: a curriculum accessed through collaborative networks, with networks populated by mobile device users who exist in a constant state of expectancy. The Net Generation are currently in our classrooms and we need to challenge the importance of recalling or just knowing facts, instead we need to offer the opportunity to build links between learning, their capacity for finding, analysing, sharing, discussing and offering critique.

They are a generation characterised as born consumers, digital natives, tech-savvy, highly social, continually connected, collaborative, multitasking, lifestyle-focused, seeking and accessing diverse media, expecting open access to everything. The web has always been part of their lives: social media, and entertainment technologies such as film, music, and games are constant components of their everyday experience.

They share their thoughts, feelings, and ideas with family and friends electronically, and they are accustomed to instantaneous information retrieval and communication. Today's students interact socially in astoundingly different ways to the generations before them.

Technology is secondary

This learning paradigm is not about the technology, which is secondary. It is about allowing us to rethink the learning relationships in every classroom. We are finding new ways of working, new ways of interacting, collaborating and sharing. Most importantly it is about the processes of 'coming to know' and 'being able to operate successfully in and across' new and ever-changing context for learning, new knowledge and learning spaces, students no longer need to go to a classroom to get information anymore.

We are already in the late desktop era. We have introduced digital learning into the classroom and, just as we are fully realising the potential for desktop technology to support learning and teaching, wired learning spaces, powerful laptops and the mobile device phenomenon is moving this technological adaptation toward obsolescence. The unwired learning space is about to significantly alter the landscape of teaching and learning with and through technology.

The ever-expanding web combined with increasingly powerful technology is offering the potential for learning opportunities that students have not been able to access before, it is informing a spirit of exploration. What it means to be knowledgeable and educated in today's world is changing. Additionally, the mobile web is opening up a host of pedagogical possibilities which will assist individuals and groups to learn anytime, anywhere.

Much has been predicted about the future of the web. I think it is safe to say that much of this transformation is already here; this evolution already surrounds us. The ability to use multimedia, and particularly social media in the context of the increasingly powerful mobile web, has become a key mode of communication – a new literacy for the 21st century.

Platforms for collaborative learning

Digital literacy is the art of using mobile technologies to enhance the learning experience. Devices continue to evolve, rapidly, as they develop into platforms for collaborative learning. We have had an explosion of new learning applications and content, demand for mobile websites has exceeded PC-accessible websites and our students can access a world of information in a moment; 'anywhere, anytime' learning is here, in and out of the classroom. Our teaching approaches need to respond in a way that more often brings focus as to how we are to make efficient use of the technologies which are increasingly familiar to our students and have the capability to increase their learning potential.

As educators we have the opportunity to bring greater significance and relevance to learning, we can develop greater awareness of why, how and what we do in our classrooms. This will inform a context which not only helps our students to understand the facts, but how the knowledge they access fits into the larger goal of learning: learning which continually informs, exercises and challenges their critical thinking skills.

In order to ensure that our students end up on the right side of the digital divide, teaching digital literacy and associated skills needs to be as crucial as teaching basic literacy. We are obliged to equip them all for the future they will inherit, one that will be continually influenced by the web. Bearing this in mind, ethically, we are called on as educators, to teach them how to use these technologies wisely and effectively.

Working in this way we will bring the best of constructivist theory to their learning as our students continually build upon their learning, collaborating and connecting in order to participate in the creation of new knowledge.

Build upon success to date

The application of new technologies can be highly motivational for our students, especially when their growing skills matrix is applied to a project-based learning context. We currently have many effective exemplars of project-based learning, we need to build upon this success as we encourage our students to more often think about what they are doing, not just focus on getting it done. In essence we need to enhance intellectual challenge and achievement by moving project-based learning from the periphery to a focal point of our curriculum experience. These elements will be student-driven, involving them in the discovery, transformation and construction of knowledge, whilst simultaneously developing new understanding and new skills.

These projects incorporate a higher degree of student autonomy, choice and lower levels of teacher direction encouraging, within our students, greater responsibility for their own learning. However we must ensure that the activities and work undertaken are realistic, embodying characteristics that give a feeling of authenticity to students, therefore developing active and contextual learning. Educators will be able to enhance students' ability to benefit from project-based learning through the introduction of scaffolding strategies intended to help students become proficient at conducting inquiry activities.

Such learning and subsequent skill development as well as gains in student achievement will be more significant and flexible than the inert knowledge that is acquired as a result of more traditional teaching approaches. If we can effectively apply and incorporate mobile technologies into the classroom, especially as a cognitive, interactive tool, we have a real opportunity to enhance the quality of students' learning.

Technology to enhance education?

As we infuse technology into our learning environments with digital learning tools and through initiatives such as Bring Your Own Device (BYOD) we will expand learning. The technology itself will become invisible in the learning process, akin to a pair of scissors; you use them when you need them. Employing technology in this way is seamless and promotes variety of new ways to learn, it fosters independent thinking, problem-solving, and collaborative learning.

These approaches will encourage personalization, accommodating students' diverse learning styles and enable them to work before or after school in ways that were not possible in the past. Essentially it allows students more control of their own learning. Teachers have the opportunity to guide more, teach less. It encourages students to seek out, to share and to build their own knowledge, truly engaging learning experiences. Teachers can provide 'scaffolding' and safety nets, providing opportunities for more student-centered learning; allowing students to explore, make mistakes, and learn from their errors. This leads to more active and interactive modes of learning.

Opportunities and potential

We need to fully understanding the huge potential of information access and to realise the myriad of opportunities it has the potential to create. The web creates a context in which information is readily available online; within our classrooms, this means factual information is potentially instantly accessible. Providing our students have the skills to navigate the web efficiently and make considered decisions as to the validity of the information presented to them, these are key skills for today's generation.

As educators we need to have the courage to demonstrate confidence in our students' ability to research independently, more often our 'not knowing' can further encourage student discovery. This needs to be applied more often and upheld as effective modelling for students. As we invite our students to utilise their skills of information access, they will develop as confident learners, further increasing their potential to participate in academic conversation.

Constantly nurturing and developing skills that will signal them as continual learners, life-long and life-wide. Furthermore, when we move into the realms of collaboration and collaborative learning, these academic conversations have the potential to extend well beyond the classroom.

As we embrace these opportunities, accepting a fundamental shift in the way students are capable of consuming and creating information (as our students begin to understand and practice using their mobile devices), we will create new and effective learning situations. The power of the mobile devices we still refer to as phones, the computing power in our pockets, can radically change not merely our classrooms but also the conversations and collaborations they have beyond our immediate sphere of influence.

Finally we arrive at the key point: most importantly we need to allow our students to have ownership of this paradigm in order that they themselves influence and continue to develop their intellectual capacity and emerge as increasingly effective and influential learners.

Students, even the very youngest, are arriving at our doors with higher levels of digital skills, able to access, communicate and collaborate; accessing the net, their learning patterns are not fixed by history, time or place. We need to connect with these skills and attitudes, with what they can do, accepting them as multi-tasking, and connected, collaborative, 21st century learners. In order to respond successfully we will need to weave digital learning opportunities into the fabric of our curriculum until they are regarded as ordinary. Events, threats and opportunities aren't just coming at us faster than ever before, they are also less predictable, converging and influencing each other to create entirely new and unforeseen paradigms.

Essentially the internet has given us connectivity, a new world of enhanced learning potential. Our lives and our learning are connected by millions of invisible threads. Which brings us to the present, we don't go to the internet anymore it surrounds us and is now an intricate part of our lives. It is imperative that we ask ourselves that as flexible, creative educators what are we capable of achieving if we truly embrace digital devices and connectivity.

To our students these technologies are trivial

Digital technologies are transforming the way we can facilitate learning for our students. To our students these technologies are trivial. Our students reach for the internet using whatever device makes sense to them at that moment. We have adopted a model for cascading skills across the Primary School; this was implemented through the introduction of Infusion Leaders within each year group. Infusion Leaders receive regular training opportunities and then share the skills they have acquired within their respective area of the school. Radiowaves, a secure social networking platform, was introduced to provide students with a means to share work in a safe and secure environment.

Bring Your Own Device (BYOD) projects and similar projects are allowing students to collaborate with great purpose. BYOD is enhancing and transforming learning through the use of technology. Technology-enhanced learning allows students to have access to educational apps and the internet, encouraging a deeper knowledge and understanding of curriculum topics and objectives. Students have the opportunity to follow individual lines of inquiry when researching on the internet with a variety of applications supporting different learning styles as they engage the brain on visual, kinaesthetic and auditory levels.

Offering students the opportunity to publish work digitally has empowered them to improve the quality of their work. It also provides a real-life purpose when creating work as they are creating digital products. Opportunities are present to embed AFL techniques in everyday lessons; students are able to use applications such as Nearpod to reflect on their learning in 'real time' with staff noting that they have witnessed higher levels of motivation, engagement and individuality in learning.

Providing alternative approaches for sharing

Augmented Reality and Quick Response codes have provided alternative approaches for sharing work with parents and the wider community. For example, Year 5 children uploaded videos to the school YouTube account and associated these videos with QR codes that were shared electronically with parents. Most importantly, our students are a source of training for teachers across our schools. In response to this as educators we need to embrace the multitude of opportunities now available to us to empower our pedagogy with digital technology, enabling our classrooms to be boundless.

"Mobile technology week was one of the highlights of the year for me. We had all the school I-pads for the week and worked on a series of challenges as a follow up to our visit to a local wildlife park. We each chose an animal we had seen and created a holiday itinerary, including flights, transfers, and accommodation bookings in order to view that animal in its natural habitat. We created an iBook to share the information on our chosen animal too. Email, photo and video, augmented reality, calendar, currency, map work were so much more fun to explore with the use of technology!" (Max, a Year 4 student).

This shift isn't coming – it's already happened. It is now.

If we are capable of, and encouraged to leave our comfort zone and focus upon developing and creating new focus for the 'how' of learning, we will redefine ourselves as potent 21st century educators. The questions we need to ask of ourselves are: Are we willing to change? Do we risk change to meet the needs of the students we serve? Because when we think we know it all, that's when the serious learning begins. It's time for us to POWER UP!

Chapter 15

Shifting sands

In the shifting sands of 21st century education everything is about context; understanding the potential benefits of the contrasting opportunities within our reach. Living in this fast-changing world producing more of the same is simply not good enough, today's students are the future, and the future depends upon their growth, their success.

We exist to help students grow

Schools and teachers exist to help students grow, learn and achieve, to discover their unique talents, and it is outstanding learning and teaching which underpins every effective school. Consequently as leaders, we need to know and understand the needs of our students and teachers futures, we need to define our direction, our vision, in order to help our learning communities to grow, succeed and meet the challenges they face.

It has been said that great teaching is easy to recognise, but hard to define, actually it is about passion as much as reason. It's also about investing in the whole system (Hargreaves & Fullan, 2012), accepting that a teacher's role is both valuable and intellectually challenging. It is our professional duty as professional leaders to identify, share and grow excellence in our schools; we move forward on the basis that there is no instant recipe for success.

Therefore, our leadership must embody and articulate our vision for great learning and teaching, to set goals, then to enable our teachers to share and achieve them to the benefit of our students. Our leadership will then offer our educators the benefit of high value, goal-orientated challenges that require action. Initial questions for us as always are: Where are we? Where are we going? How will we get there? Where to next?

Leaders anticipate the future

As effective leaders we continually anticipate the future, a future which is always under construction! Accepting this challenge, our leadership should always be pushing the envelope, demonstrating that we know what excellent teaching looks like, including what excellent teachers know and do. That said the defining factor affecting our progress would always be the human factor, to assure success we need to identify, to employ and to empower educators who will be the wind beneath our wings, who will realize new levels of success.

The individual contribution of each and every member of our teams will play a key role in shaping positive futures for our schools and ultimately, every one of our students. We need educators with high aspiration and expectation, great interpersonal and team skills, task-orientated with the determination to become reflective, expert thinkers.

Within our schools, we foster 'organisational learning' building the capacity of the school for high performance and continuous improvement, for excellence. In maintaining the challenge of continuous improvement, we acknowledge the power of great teachers, the power of learning intentions, the power of literacy, because literacy is the cornerstone of student achievement.

This paradigm has far reaching consequences for us as school leaders as we encourage students to embrace learning and cultural diversity in our global society. We need to take experiences to our students that will allow them to learn in ways that are conducive to their personal and intellectual growth, and literacy lies at the heart of this. Strategies to promote and remediate literacy figure prominently in our thinking, as literacy is the foundation of student achievement. With regard to skills development and student competence in this field we live in a world which has an ever increasing demand from and focus upon literacy skills.

Of course great progress has been made but, 'It's no use saying 'we are doing our best'. You have got to succeed in doing what is necessary'. (Sir Winston Churchill)

We make a significant difference

Until the 1960s the view was that schools make almost no difference to student achievement. Today we know that teachers, learning and schools make a significant difference to student success, we know how teacher expertise develops, and we also know what good teaching looks like.

However, we are also aware that teacher quality varies within and across schools. In setting a clear focus for the future, a quality teacher in every classroom is our ultimate aim, but how to achieve this is a big question. This massive challenge entails continually maintaining positive relationships and building people, this is critical as the most important factor affecting student learning is the teacher. Therefore the greatest difference we can make within our school is to improve the effectiveness of our teachers. How then are we prioritising teacher development? How are we to enhance our teachers?

Making best practice common practice

Our task is to make best practice, common practice. Our message to our teachers is that they need to be active agents of their own professional development: life-long learners. We need to maintain a clear focus upon student learning, achievement and progress, provide active and high quality teaching, we can only do this through professional learning, and highly focussed leadership. According to Hattie (2009), the major sources of variance in student achievement are the students themselves (50%) and teachers (30%). It is what teachers know, do, and care about which is very powerful in this learning equation.

The value of great teachers cannot be underestimated but they themselves need to be inspired and excited about the purpose of their professional lives. The teacher and the quality of teaching are the major influences on student achievement, along with the individual student and his or her prior achievement.

Great teachers know their students well, have high expectations for all, they know what they can do and what they can't do yet! Great teaching occurs when these educators bring focussed learning intentions and success criteria, then makes them transparent to the students and demonstrate by modelling. Effective teachers will then evaluate student understanding, discovering if what they had been told has made sense to them, checking for understanding, and if necessary, reiterating what has been told, tying it all together with a focused learning plenary. An expert teacher, readily explains, demonstrates and detects flaws in learning outcomes. They also identify talent and potential, and build upon them. (Dinham, 2008)

Being student-centered and teacher-directed

Great lessons are most often student-centered and teacher-directed, with teachers being highly responsive to students as well as being highly demanding. These lessons have a clear emphasis on students thinking, problem-solving and the application of knowledge. Understanding is built in layers, with connections to previous learning with teachers continually offering mutual respect, nurturing confidence and setting high expectations. Key features are timely and constructive assessment, early, appropriate intervention and feedback, challenging students to reach beyond the demands of the National Curriculum, or any scheme of work, creating environments of possibility.

Rigor and reflection are also key with teachers questioning outcomes as follows: Did they learn what they were supposed to learn? Did they retain it over time? Can they use it in ways that demonstrate understanding at a high level?

We know teaching to be a demanding, complex, dynamic activity, highly dependent on personal relationships and professional judgement. The best teachers are genuinely expert in their area; they enjoy teaching offering joy and passion for learning. Aligning our learning and teaching with external standards allows us to set goals for increased performance which are ambitious, achievable and measurable. Goal setting creates a context where we will be able to integrate external and internal accountability, against the background of agreed learning goals and performance outcomes, continually moving our teachers and our schools forward.

Teacher development requires team-based professional learning, sharing resources, teaching paradigms, setting high expectations, consistency and joint initiatives. We need to grasp the value of deliberate practice. For deliberate practice to work teachers must have a deep desire to succeed. This is fundamental because this is an investment of time energy and knowledge: it means effort now, benefits later. Deliberate practice includes performance that is based on a particular element of the task, expert coaching, feedback, careful and accurate self-assessment, and the opportunity to apply feedback immediately for improved performance (Reeves, 2010). The development of an inspirational, expert teacher requires that you practice deliberately, with focused feedback, always seeking to enhance and improve upon your current situation, continually progressing. At no time should we underestimate the value and the importance of feedback to learning and individual accomplishment.

Creating a positive, 'can do' culture

As 21st-century educators and leaders, we must be fluid thinkers, ready to look at situations with fresh, creative eyes. We must go beyond the ordinary to empower all students to learn, to question, to create, to discuss, to rethink, to imagine and to collaborate (*Quality teaching Matters*, Dinham). We need to motivate students, allowing them to take charge of their learning by helping them to understand where they are and how they can move forward. To achieve this it is necessary to articulate high aspirations, expectations and achievement, creating a positive 'can-do' culture.

Our key target is for each student to have great teachers and quality learning within and across our schools supported by effective leadership and professional learning in a mutually respectful environment. In essence, excellent teachers respond to challenges through reflecting, growing and adapting the way they teach, demonstrating their capability to develop their practice and our curriculum to meet the needs of our students, teaching them the things they really need to know.

As engaged leaders we can promote collaboration and teamwork amongst our educators within and across schools, engage in developmental teacher monitoring offering high level coaching and evaluation which will continually inform professional development. Our aim being to develop a collaborative school where all of the teachers take pride in their and all of the students' achievements and work together to do whatever it takes to meet the goals of our students. This is only possible with engaged teachers committed to their work and reflecting on their own teaching to become the better educators that they thought they could be.

As effective leaders we must assert the discretion we have to set strategic direction for our schools setting goals, continually monitoring progress, encouraging teachers to be active agents in their own progress and that of the school. Great leadership is essential to promote, support and sustain the drive to constantly develop and improve and to strive to maximise learning potential in our schools.

Finally, we know that teaching takes time to master and that great teachers are constantly re-inventing themselves. Success, over time, will be a series of small wins built upon the wings of hope and encouragement. We can encourage our educators toward a greater future as they are continue to face new contexts and challenges against a background of no two days, and no two lessons, ever being the same.

Quality teaching matters and it's time we started acting like it (Dinham, Ingvarson & Kleinhenz, 2008).

References and further reading

Dinham, S., Ingvarson, L. & Kleinhenz, E. (2008) *Teaching talent: the best teachers for Australia's classrooms.* Melbourne: Business Council of Australia

Dinham, S. (2008) *How to Get Your School Moving and Improving.* Camberwell Vic: ACER Press

Dweck, C. (2000): *Self-Theories – Their Role in Motivation, Personality and Development.* Philadelphia, PA: Psychology Press

Hargreaves & Fullan, 2012: *Professional Capital.* New York: Teachers College Press

Hattie, J. (2009) *Visible Learning – A synthesis of over 800 meta-analyses relating to achievement.* London: Routledge

Reeves, D. (2010) *Transforming Professional Development into Student Results.* Alexandria, Va.: ASCD

The Restless School

By Roy Blatchford

What do successful schools and their leaders have in common? They are restless. There is a paradox at their core: they are very secure in their systems, values and successes, yet simultaneously seeking to change and improve. These schools look inwards to secure wise development; they look outwards to seize innovation which they can hew to their own ends and, importantly, make a difference to the children and students they serve. That is the restless school.

"In this thought-provoking book Roy Blatchford draws on 40 years of wide ranging experience within the UK and international education systems in order to capture the essence of successful schools."

Brian Lightman, Association of School and College Leaders

"Blatchford sets teachers, schools and their leaders a standard that's terrifying in prospect, yet assuredly attainable if we can just maintain our courage, commitment and determination - our professionalism, indeed, as he stresses. Inspired by this remarkable small handbook of school excellence, I don't see how we can avoid accepting and confronting the challenge. It would be rude not to!"

Bernard Trafford, Headmaster, Royal Grammar School, Newcastle

"I wish I had read The Restless School in the early days of my teaching - indeed at any stage of my teaching. In a short and pacy book I found distilled everything that matters, all expressed in a generous, open and wise way. And it puts a spring in your step."

Jonathan Smith, author of The Learning Game

Roy Blatchford is Director of the National Education Trust. Previously he was Her Majesty's Inspector of Schools in England, with national responsibilities for school improvement and for the inspection of outstanding schools.

He is the author/editor of over 150 books and is a regular contributor to the national media. Recent books include Sparkling Classrooms, The 2012 Teachers Standards and Taking Forward the Primary Curriculum.

Lightning Source UK Ltd.
Milton Keynes UK
UKOW06f0141280715

255938UK00003B/90/P